D1628121

Shelson

It's Amazing

What You Can Learn

When You Can Read!

Magdalene Wilson

ISBN: 0-9724370-0-2

FIRST EDITION

For Mary Lee Killingbeck
October 20, 1948 - August 22, 1998

In loving memory of the original and long-serving Executive Director of the Dyslexia Resource Center. It was her mission and passion to serve dyslexics and their families. Her dream of making a difference in people's lives was realized. It shall live on forever with her wisdom and guidance from above.

CONTENTS

Introduction
Batches
Chapter 1	1
Chapter 2	8
Chapter 3	17
Chapter 4	21
Chapter 5	32
Chapter 6	41
Chapter 7	47
Chapter 8	56
Informational
Chapter 9	62
Chapter 10	71
For Parents
Chapter 11	78
For Educators
Chapter 12	93
For College Students
Chapter 13	102
Visual Tool
Chapter 14	106
Epilogue	108

INTRODUCTION

I am writing this book because I want to reach parents. Parents who ask themselves, 'Why can't my intelligent child learn to read?' Parents who watch their child try and try to do school work, but fail. Parents who feel powerless as they watch their child's self-esteem slowly erode away. Parents who are searching for answers. Parents who feel guilty, who go to bed every night frustrated. It took me twenty years to stop feeling guilt. My only regret is that I didn't have this information thirty years ago, that my son didn't start learning at a young age, and avoid the trauma he experienced. I want to reach as many parents as possible. I want parents to be informed, so they'll know how to help their children.

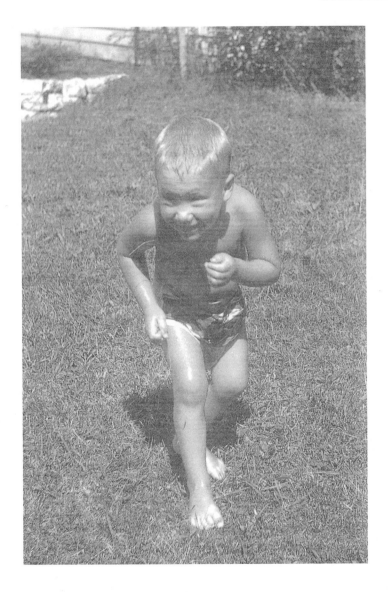

CHAPTER 1

How do I begin? Where do I start? How do I tell my story, so others can learn from my experiences? How do I share a part of my heart and soul, to give hope to others? I want to begin with a tow-headed, green-eyed, all legs and arms little boy, who loved to rough and tumble with the neighbor's dachshunds, in the back yard of our small home. A mother's pride and joy, a very inquisitive little boy who embraced life with open arms, a child who loved to play. A happy time, before society's "norms" would make me painfully aware that he was different, and the guilt would begin. Guilt, my self-imposed burden.

Guilt leads me back further, to a doctor's office in a small town in Ohio. I was a young mother of one, and my doctor was informing me that he was going on vacation, and therefore, needed to move the date of the cesarean delivery of my second child ahead, three and onehalf weeks before the baby was due to arrive. I thought, "That's not right, babies need to go full-term. They shouldn't be brought into this world early; something might happen. They might not start to breathe; they might not be fully developed. What do I do? I can't start labor again, as I did with my first child, I just can't go through all that, and then have to go through surgery like the first time." So with great concern, and much hesitation, I agreed to let the doctor deliver my baby three and onehalf weeks early. In 1952 a woman didn't argue with her doctor.

My beautiful baby boy seemed perfect when they handed him to me, after I awakened from the surgery. He weighed over five pounds, which was a good birth weight. The doctor told me he was fine.

Still, had this been the reason? Had my baby not started breathing at delivery? Had something gone wrong? No one would have told me if it had, not in 1952. Had my decision caused his problems? These thoughts haunted my mind over the years. Guilt, a constant companion.

Then again, could it have been the trauma I experienced during my seventh month of pregnancy? My in-laws had come to visit their only grandchild. I knew that Grandpa was terribly depressed, and needed help. I didn't realize how much, because Grandma had never told us what had been going on at home. She didn't even discuss it with my husband, her son.

While my young son played with his Grandma in the living room, I was busy making lunch in the kitchen. Deciding to serve canned peaches, I went carefully down the basement stairs. As I turned the corner toward the canned goods shelf, I saw my father-in-law fully exposing his genitals. Shocked, I whirled around and ran back up the stairs, as quickly as a seven and a half month pregnancy would allow. Stunned and upset, I didn't know what to do. I could not cope with the situation, so acted like nothing out of the ordinary had happened. I said nothing to my husband, just finished making lunch, without the peaches. Yet, could this awful stress have injured my baby in some way?

My in-laws were to go home the next day. I told my husband, without revealing the reason, that he should take his father back, and get him some psychological counseling, because I felt he was having terrible emotional problems. My husband said his dad would be okay; he had work at the office he needed to get done. Two days later, my mother-in-law called me, not her son, to let me know that Grandpa had hanged himself in the basement of their home. This was another traumatic experience for me. I should have insisted that Grandpa get the help he desperately needed.

Then, there was the funeral. My husband was an only child; it fell on him to make all the arrangements. My husband did not talk to me about his childhood. I can only surmise that he was not happy. He would withdraw from unpleasant or unwanted reality. He would pretend the pain wasn't there, and put his energy into things that made him happy. I was emotionally stronger, and did what needed to be done. My doctor offered to give me tablets for the stress, but I didn't think that I was so upset that I needed medication. However, it was terribly difficult to listen to friends say, "Why did he do such a thing?" They couldn't understand it. I sat there knowing the reason, saying nothing. Had this stress and trauma affected the child I was carrying?

Or maybe it was the time when he was two years old. Our family was traveling by car, to Ohio, in December. We had moved to Michigan. As we drove along, my son started to have convulsions from a high fever. Quickly, I took off his coat, opened the vent in the window, and placed his face to the vent, hoping to cool him down. We stopped at the next store and I bought baby aspirin to give to him. I didn't have a thermometer with me. How high had his temperature gotten? Was it high enough to cause brain damage? Did I cool him down quickly enough? Should we have gone to the hospital? These were painful questions, with elusive answers.

When my child's problems began, when he started reading in the first grade, and for many years after, these thoughts raced through my mind, many, many times. Guilt, ..hat had I caused?

My feeling was one of being totally absorbed with my son's problems. I felt that my child was the only child to

3

suffer this way. I now know that's not how it is. That is why I have to write this book.

* * * *

His name is Batches, a nickname given to him by his family and friends. Perhaps it was the way his shoes were always untied, or his shirt always hung out because he had such small hips, or the way he used to tumble and roll, then pop right back up on his feet, or the way he collected dirt, as some children do. I can't remember exactly why, but it stuck.

The day Batches had been excitedly waiting for, finally arrived, his first day of kindergarten. He was bright-eyed and ready to go to school, just like his older brother. He skipped off, down the street, ready to start a new adventure. Batches already knew his ABC's; he knew how to count, not to 100 yet, but he could count to 10 and was rather proud of that fact. He made some new friends; he loved art and drawing. Kindergarten went well, Batches fully enjoyed school.

* * * *

Looking back, there were a couple of things I did notice when Batches was in kindergarten. He could not repeat back to me, the days of the week in order: Monday, Tuesday, Wednesday, Thursday, Friday, Saturday, Sunday. He would say: Tuesday, Wednesday, Saturday, Thursday, Friday, Sunday, Monday. This was equally true with the months of the year. I tried to teach him the Spring months, and then the Fall months, but it didn't work. He knew the names, but he could not put them in the right order. I later learned, this is called sequencing difficulty.

Batches had trouble knowing his right and his left. One day after school, he decided to find his older brother who was playing at a friend's house. Batches had walked there before with his older brother but knew he wasn't allowed to go by himself. However, on that afternoon, when I went outside to check on him, he wasn't in our yard. I walked up and down our street, calling his name, but there was no response. When his older brother came home I anxiously asked, "Have you seen Batches?" "No mom, I haven't," he told me. By now it was beginning to get dark and Batches had been gone for two hours. The worried, awful, helpless feeling started. I knew that young man of mine had taken off to walk to the house, where his older brother had gone to play.

My stomach was in knots, I called the police, this was every mother's nightmare of having their precious child missing. I decided to take one more look up and down our street. When I glanced to my right, here came a little boy in his dark-blue snowsuit, and red stocking hat, trudging along in a very, very tired manner.

I didn't know whether to spank him or pick him up and hug him. I was so upset with him, and at the same time thankful he was safe. He looked so tired, he had been walking all that time, trying to find his way. I said, "Batches, were you lost?" "Yeah Mom," Batches said, "I tried to find Lee's house and I got lost. I couldn't find my way home and I walked and I walked. All of a sudden I could see this gas station, when I looked down the street. The same gas station at the street where I live. That's how I found my way back."

At that moment I picked this tired little boy up in my arms, gave him a big hug, and carried him home.

To this day, Batches never goes anywhere, unless he knows exactly how he's going to get there, and how he's going to get back home. Time and again, I have seen him use a map to figure out exactly the routes he needs to take, the numbers of those routes, so that he never again gets lost. This incident must have been very traumatic for my little son.

* * * *

Batches was looking forward to another good year at school when summer vacation ended, and first grade began. However, first grade was a different story; it was a real struggle. Batches was having difficulty learning to read. I bought a set of flashcards. The first time through the set of flashcards, Batches could only identify the word 'cat.' The next time through he could only identify the word 'me.' He had forgotten the word 'cat.' And so it went. We worked and we worked with the flashcards.

I didn't know at the time, that flashcards were not the way to teach this little boy to read. I learned this so much later. I have also learned that today, we would have called Batches, "a child at risk to learn." There are many children who are not developmentally ready to learn to read. I felt Batches was one of them. He started school at a young age, he turned five in late August. His teachers at school conferences would say, "He's a boy, he's young, he's just not ready to learn. He will begin to learn when he is developmentally ready." I knew these difficulties were

6

sometimes due to immaturity, especially in boys. Many boys do not mature as fast as girls in learning language skills.

Batches struggled on. The end of first grade came, and a very sad little boy brought his final grade card home. On it were the words, REPEAT FIRST GRADE. Children can be cruel, "Hah, Batches has to go back to first grade. Batches didn't pass." These taunts echoed in his head as he walked the long mile home. And a sad little boy said, "I have to take first grade over, Mom."

I went along with the teacher's recommendations which, as I look back, was a big mistake. The next year came, and the flashcards started all over again. His teachers taught reading, using the 'see and say' method. Each child is expected to LOOK at a word; SEE it; SAY it; and LEARN it. But not my little boy and not other children who learn differently. Batches only wasted another whole year of his life. The emotional upheaval of repeating first grade, and still not learning to read, affected his self esteem.

Batches told me many years later, it was at this point in his life, when he had to repeat first grade, that he felt he was different from everyone else. He felt "different" all through school, because his school experience did nothing to alleviate this feeling, only reinforce it.

CHAPTER 2

Batches moved on to second grade. The teacher was dedicated, a good teacher. His father and I had chosen the area to live, based on the excellent reputation of the school system. The community was made up largely of professionals. Education for our children was important. My husband and I both graduated from the university.

In March, I had another parent teacher conference. Another conference with no hope of finding answers to the difficulty Batches had in learning to read. During this meeting, his teacher said to me, "There's something wrong here. When I talk with Batches, he knows everything. When his papers come in, nothing is right."

Unknowingly, this second grade teacher had pin-pointed the problem, Inability to grasp the written English language. Batches was capable, however, of learning the English language in an oral manner. What the teacher did not realize at that time was excellent oral language, poor reading and written language were the essence of Batches' language problem.

The teacher suggested, after speaking with a psychologist at the local university, that we set up an appointment for Batches to have an EEG taken at the Caro State Hospital for Epileptics and the Mentally Retarded. She felt there was the possibility of brain damage or emotional trauma.

Since Batches was still struggling with his class work, especially reading, and his math was beginning to be involved, his father and I decided that we needed to follow the recommendation of the teacher.

I lay awake that night thinking about what Batches' teacher had said, 'brain damage.' I thought about all the things that could have caused my son to have brain damage. High fever; early birth; traumatic pregnancy. Which one had caused it? How could I have stopped it from happening? What would I tell my son?

Batches was nine years old the summer of 1961. Caro State Hospital is near a lake, and so I planned a family outing. Batches would have the EEG done in the early afternoon and then spend the rest of the day at the lake, swimming and having a picnic.

The EEG was no problem; Batches cooperated well. I was with him as they attached the wires to his head. Batches looked over all the equipment in the lab. He didn't seem scared. He was interested in what was going on around him. I went home with no premonition, unaware of the terrible consequences this report would have on my son's life.

* * * *

To make things clearer, I'm going to give you information that wasn't available to me at that time. A copy of the report from Caro State Hospital was automatically sent to Batches' school, and remained a part of his academic record. His father and I never received a copy of this report. Twenty-one years later, I read the summary of that report, "This boy presents evidence of mental retardation." (These were the shocking, unbelievable words I read.) "The neurological examination is otherwise negative. The findings of the EEG are non-specific and there is certainly no clinical evidence of epilepsy at this time. It appears that his management should be based on his intellectual capacity."

9

This diagnosis was made only on the fact that Batches read two years below grade level. With my health education background, when I was finally able to peruse this report, I found, they really didn't know specifically what they were seeing. They were ignorant psychologists who had not been versed in nor researched the problems involved in the teaching and the learning of reading.

Thus, they placed this very wrong diagnosis on the school record, of a young boy, in the second year of his schooling. It followed him all though his academic career. How many other children have been wrongly diagnosed in our educational system? It's painful to comprehend.

* * * *

Batches' difficulties at school continued. We had him privately tutored, by a lovely, elderly lady who had a degree in teacher education. As a young girl, she had broken her back, and wasn't physically able to teach full-time. She tutored children, and worked with the handicapped at a local school. We thought perhaps she could help. She would know how to go about teaching him. She really liked Batches. She would tell me, "He works so hard and concentrates so very well." Batches would faithfully go to tutoring and tried really hard to learn. Sometimes he would say to me, "Why do I have to go, everyone else is out playing," but he went. The problem was that she was tutoring him, exactly the same way the schools were teaching him during the day. He couldn't learn in that way. We finally stopped going because I could see it was not the answer to the problems Batches had in school.

* * * *

When Batches was in the third grade, he stopped to play with a friend after school. Kids being kids, he decided to climb a tree. It was in the Fall, after all the leaves had fallen to the ground. Batches fell and broke the two bones above his left wrist. The mother of the boy where he was playing was an alcoholic and her son couldn't awaken her from a nap. Batches was about a half mile from home, so holding his arm tight against himself, he walked home. He came in the back door and calmly said, "Mom, I broke my arm. I fell out of a tree." I peeked up the sleeve of his fall coat and immediately saw the one bone had penetrated the skin. How painful that long walk must have been! I quickly sat him down and called his doctor.

Batches' pediatrician took him right in, took one look and told me to take him immediately to the orthopedic doctor. He gave Batches a shot for pain and we were on our way. The orthopedic doctor said it was so bad Batches would have to go to the hospital to have anesthetic before the bones could be set. When he told me this, I realized what grit it must have taken for Batches to walk that distance home. As I drove him to the hospital he told me, "I didn't realize the limb was dead, Mom, because all the leaves were off. When I stepped on it, it gave way and when (my friend) couldn't wake up his mom, I knew I had to get home so you could take care of me." As I look back on that incident, and then think about Caro State Hospital's report, I don't see a "mentally retarded" little boy. I see a highly intelligent little boy, able to size up a difficult situation and choose the best course to follow. Oh how I wish I had been given the results of that EEG report from Caro State Hospital.

* * * *

Batches' father more or less ignored Batches because he sensed that he was different from our other three children. His dad never wanted to face any problems. He just wanted everything to be fine. I felt the whole burden of Batches' problems were on me, as I had no emotional support or educational support, nothing. Sometimes it was overwhelming; Batches' frustration became my frustration. My guilt grew more profound with his increasing problems with school. I felt very inadequate when I tried to teach him to read and write.

* * * *

It was a spring day, when Batches was in the fifth grade, and he'd come home for lunch. All the kids were sitting around the table eating their sandwiches when suddenly Batches asked me, "Mom, why did you take me up to that place that time? That place where they put all those wires on my head and they did those things that you said were a test." I was not ready for a question like that, right out of the blue. How do I explain to my son in a way in which he would understand that I knew and believed he could learn? I told him the truth. I said, "Remember your second grade teacher? Well, she suggested that there might be a problem with your being able to learn to read. So we took you to that hospital to find out. It is not a problem, you are able to learn, Batches. Your father and I just wanted to be sure you weren't having any problems." Batches seemed satisfied with my answer, but I couldn't help wondering if something had happened at school to trigger that question.

After Batches went back to school that day, I started thinking about that test at Caro. I asked myself, 'What had I really learned?' His father and I had held a meeting with the psychiatric consultants from the local university. I had questioned them at the time, "What did you find?" "Well we aren't sure what we found," was the evasive answer. "Well, what's the problem," I asked. "Well, um, we really aren't sure," was the response. "Well, what do you foresee for my son?" I asked. "Well, we feel he will be able to learn as much as he is capable of learning," they replied. I suddenly realized, they had avoided telling me exactly what was on that report.

Why on earth didn't they tell me then, what those psychologists and medical personnel at Caro had put on my son's records? Because as a mother and a former teacher, I would have known that report was ABSOLUTELY NOT TRUE. At that point, I would have had my child retested, and I feel that I might have found someone, with the knowledge to have helped Batches. I was beyond angry when I finally got to read that report in 1982 and I saw what they had written. I had to come to grips with the realization of what this had done to my son. Words cannot describe my pain. If only they had been honest with me and told me the truth. For this I can never forgive them!

* * * *

It was time for another parent teacher conference, sixth grade this time. I was told by Batches' teacher, "Batches is doing things he really shouldn't be able to do. I think you should have another examination, another report on his problem. I feel that the one we have is not correct." I still

13

did not know what the report from Caro said. The State would not allow you to obtain that kind of information at that time. So unknowingly, I made a second huge mistake.

The father of a friend with whom Batches played was a well known psychologist. I asked this psychologist what his impression of Batches was. He said, "Oh he's doing fine." Of course, this parent saw Batches outside an educational setting, talking normally, playing normally. Doing all the normal things a child would do. He hadn't observed him in a classroom. It was a mistake to depend on that opinion.

But at the time I thought, 'Well, this psychologist says Batches is okay, he's doing alright.' I let it go. A big factor, that affected my decision, was our family's financial inability to pay the cost of another evaluation.

* * * *

Batches hated the crows nest. He was sent there every year from the second grade to the sixth grade. Every morning for an hour he would work with the special reading teacher. He hated it. His classroom teacher would say, "Batches, it is time for you to go." And he would get up, in front of the whole class and head out for the crows nest. Down the aisle, and past his friends. Feeling all eyes on him, that everyone was looking at him. Everyone knowing he couldn't read. Feeling extremely inadequate, and very terribly stupid, he would head out the door to the crows nest.

It was the old superintendent's office. The elementary school had been restructured from a high school. The crows nest sat alone at the top of a special set of stairs that descended from the second floor. The children, who had problems learning to read, went there. "The place where stupid kids went," was how Batches later described it.

His special reading teacher was very caring, very nice. She had a degree in teacher education and was certified as a specialist to teach reading. The problem was that she had not been taught about Batches' learning style. She didn't realize she was teaching him in a way that he could not learn. She may have heard some bits of information, for instance, auditory processing problems, visual processing problems, and short-term memory. However, she had not been taught in college how to teach children like Batches how to read.

Don't misunderstand me, I'm not blaming Batches' reading teacher because she could not teach him to read. It wasn't her fault. I'm putting the blame squarely on the colleges of education. I say this with much anger. The colleges have not taught their students how to teach these different learners to read, write and spell.

Batches' special reading teacher told me when he was in the sixth grade, that when she read to Batches he was able to comprehend and understand ninth grade reading material. When she gave him this same material to read for himself, he couldn't do it. That in itself should have told her that she had a very intelligent boy, who could not learn by the way he was being taught. Again, here was one of the typical examples of persons like Batches.

Every year from the second grade to the sixth grade, everyday of school at a certain time, "Batches, it is time for you to go." Do you know what this did to my intelligent young son? All those years of frustration, anger, pain and destruction of self-image. He never told me how much he hated it, not until later.

Children like Batches are intelligent. They are not mentally retarded. They learn differently. They know that they are not learning what they ought to be learning. They question why. Many emotional problems are the result of the way that schools are teaching these children.

CHAPTER 3

Junior High was a disaster. I knew he was in a special class with Mrs. Brown, but Batches never told me that his classes were held in the old furnace room of the Junior High School. Batches was in a class with children whom the school had labeled, unable to learn. With students who did not want to be in school, who were truant much of the time. With students who had emotional problems and students who were discipline problems. The teacher spent most of her time managing her classroom, maintaining discipline. Learning was not taking place in this environment.

How many other children in this classroom were like Batches? How many were hiding behind their own 'masks?' How many other students in this classroom could have been helped, along with Batches?

Basically, what Batches learned in Junior High was how to respect his teachers and not cause trouble. With this new found knowledge, Batches quietly began to withdraw. Back of the room—teacher won't notice me—don't volunteer—then no one will know how stupid I am—just learn all I can by listening.

At the time, the school had told me that Batches was going to be placed in Mrs. Brown's classroom where he would get special help. Other parents had told me what a great teacher she was. I thought the reason Batches never brought any papers home from his English, Math or Science classes was because Mrs. Brown was helping him with his school work.

Batches was too embarrassed, too ashamed to tell his mother that he was being taught in the old furnace room at school. He didn't tell me that he stayed in Mrs. Brown's classroom all day long. He hated that class. I never knew the truth until years later when he talked to me about all his experiences at school.

No wonder there were times when Batches wouldn't listen to anybody. There were days when he wouldn't listen at all, to anything I asked him to do. He was so frustrated and angry with the way he was being treated at school. He was continuously questioning his ability to learn. These are the times when these children need to be hugged. Taken in your arms, hugged and told that they are loved. When they are the most unlovable, they need you to be the most loving.

* * * *

Batches often had trouble explaining situations to other people. Especially people with whom he was not familiar, strangers. Once Batches decided to ride his brother's new ten-speed bike downtown. Unfortunately, at this time, bicycles were being stolen in large numbers in our town. As Batches was riding the bike, a policeman spotted him. Batches was smaller than his older brother, so the bike was too big for him. The policeman obviously knew the bike wasn't his, he stopped Batches to question him.

Batches was so unsure of himself by this time, it was difficult for him to talk to strangers. Thus he did what most children with these problems will do; he blocked. He could not orally say what he wanted to say to the policeman. The policeman became even more suspicious. Batches finally asked him to come home with him so that he could prove it was his brother's bike.

I answered a knock at the door. There stood a policeman with Batches in tow. Batches explained, "Mom, tell the policeman that I was riding my brother's bike. He won't believe me." I said, "Of course, that's his brother's bike. He had permission to ride it." The policeman was a little embarrassed. However, he didn't apologize to Batches. He turned on his heel and went back to his patrol car.

* * * *

I remember another incident in my young son's life, and this had to do with my church, of all places. I had gone to our young minister and told him that Batches had difficulty reading, writing and spelling. I said I would appreciate it if Batches could just audit the catechism class. The minister agreed.

I drove him to catechism once a week. He had been enrolled for about three or four weeks. When we got ready to leave for catechism that fifth week, Batches stopped me and said, "Mom, I'm not going to catechism. Two weeks ago the minister handed out essay tests and we were supposed to take them, even me. I tried to tell him that I couldn't do this, but he insisted that I write what I could. I handed in a blank piece of paper. I'm not going back, Mom. The last two weeks I've gone into church and then after you drive off, I come back out and walk around town until I know catechism class is over. Then I walk home."

I was stunned. When his older brother had been in catechism and he missed one class, I got a call from the church immediately saying, "Where is he, he should be in class." Suddenly, it dawned on me that the minister had not called me when Batches had missed the class, because he had written Batches off as a person, unable to learn.

After this happened I had difficulty attending church, in fact I left the church for almost two years. I kept in touch with God in my own way. I eventually did return to church, but not to that minister. To this day, Batches rarely goes to church. He was raised in a Christian home and he has good moral values. Sadly, when its Sunday and I say, "I'm going to Church today Batches. Won't you come with me?" His response is usually the same, "No Mom. No way."

* * * *

There was one good memory for Batches in junior high. He began playing football. The physical education teacher came to me and said, "Batches is probably the most outstanding athlete I have ever had in my classes." And it was true. Batches could run like a deer. Athletics became an outlet for his frustrations at what was happening to him in the classroom. This is where Batches found success, something he could feel good about. At the same time, I'm not sure that it wasn't partly his undoing. Educators focused on his athletic abilities and conveniently swept his other problems under the carpet.

CHAPTER 4

High School was difficult. Batches turned to his athletic successes in football. It was his life-saver in one way, his downfall in another. Because of his football ability, his teachers gave him C's. Because of a report that haunted him through the grades and labeled him "mentally retarded," his teachers gave him C's. I'm sure the teachers thought they were doing Batches a favor, handing him C's. After all he could probably get a job with General Motors working on the line. High School wrote him off. He did C average work right? Wrong. But his report card said he did. A job on the line of an automobile plant is a decent job, but I did not want Batches pigeon-holed into a job by society at the age of sixteen. Choice is very important, I wanted Batches to be given the opportunity to shape his own future.

* * * *

I went to every high school teacher he had, every year, during the Fall Parent/Teacher Open House, and asked the same question, "Can Batches please use a tape-recorder in your classroom to tape his classes?" I did not know at the time that this was his right, that the teachers could not deny my request. However, the teachers response to my question was always the same, "I don't want to have my classes taped." They didn't want a parent listening to what happened in their classroom. I could not convince them, that his father and I would not be listening to the tapes, that the tapes would only be used by Batches. Batches couldn't take notes in class because he couldn't spell, and he couldn't read his textbook.

* * * *

Batches had another unfavorable run in with a policeman in high school. It happened a few days after Batches took his Driver's Ed written exam at the High School. A driver's license is an important rite of passage in a young man's life. I had worked with him, and I knew that he was ready for his driver's license written exam. A few days after the exam we went to the local police station to get the results.

Batches and I walked up to the counter, and the policeman behind the counter looked his test over. In a not very pleasant tone he said, "He needs to go home and study. He doesn't know any of this." Batches' face fell. I held on to my temper and said very quietly to the officer, "Do you mind if I see the test?" He handed me the test, I looked it over. The first page, and half-way down the second page, everything was right. The rest of the questions were all marked wrong. We left the police station.

After getting in the car I said to my son, "What happened Batches?" He said, "A policeman passed out the tests at school and then sat there watching us. Of course everybody else finished their test and left. I was the last one there. The policeman sat at the desk for a while, then he began to tap his pencil on the desk, then he came and started walking up and down by my desk, as if to say, 'Why aren't you done? What's going on?'

Batches didn't need to tell me any more. This was exactly what my son did not need. When you put pressure on people like Batches the way the policeman did, the processing of the brain just stops. He couldn't concentrate. He couldn't read. The words wouldn't come.

As I looked at him as I was driving home, I saw all his emotions clearly written on his face. He was not just angry. He was mad at himself, mad at the world. He had wanted that driver's license with all his heart. When I arrived home, I was really upset. I called my sister and told her what had happened. She said, "You take him out to the county sheriff's office. That's where my girls went. The woman at the desk gave them the test, and they had all the time in the world to complete it." Batches was so upset that this was worth a try.

Back to the car we went, ten miles out to the county sheriff's office. Batches again went through the testing. The woman there gave Batches the test, and seated him in a chair, in a corner by himself. Then she watched him out of the corner of her eye as she went about her work. No pressure.

I must admit that I sat and sat and sat. An hour passed, an hour and one-half. I glanced over at where he was sitting and could see that he was going back and turning the pages and checking things over. Patience.

Batches walked up to the desk with his completed test. The woman checked it over with her score key. Batches had missed only two questions, because he had been given time to process what he was reading, with no outside pressure.

The impatience of the policeman, who had given Batches his first Driver's Ed exam, had caused him to fail. The policeman's inappropriate actions insured failure. Batches should have been allowed to quietly take his test, with no time limits, that were either set or imagined by the officer.

The sheriff took Batches out to the car for the road test. When they returned the officer told me, "He's a good driver."

Batches was happy as a lark. He bounded out of the sheriff's office with his permit and whipped in behind the wheel. I could have kissed my sister for suggesting that I bring Batches out to the sheriff's office to retake his Driver's Education test.

* * * *

When Batches was a Junior, he went to a party one Friday night. The kind of party all kids that age go to. A friend had a bunch of kids over to their house to listen to music, talk, and party. Sitting at a table was a girl doing a cross-word puzzle with her friends. She looked up and said to everyone gathered around, "If Batches can spell this word I'll eat the paper." Another painful put-down from his peers.

Batches' good friend Bill stepped in. He leaned over the cross-word puzzle, pointed to a word and said to the girl, "If you can tell me what this word means, I'll eat the paper." The girl couldn't.

Bill was trying to protect his friend. But the damage was done. You don't gain self-worth from having others fight your battles for you.

* * * *

Batches told me, years later, about his freshmen math class. He was stood up in class on a regular basis and made an example of, because he had not worked on or finished his homework. He was sent to the chalkboard at the front of the classroom and was embarrassed, humiliated, by his math teacher. I suppose his math teacher felt Batches' lack of math knowledge was attributed to the lack of homework completed, lack of studying. If he humiliated Batches enough, the homework would get done. Right? Wrong. That is a common misperception by teachers. These students in our schools are so misunderstood.

I had no idea this was happening to him. I get so angry every time I think about how miserable this teacher made my son's life. Being stood up in front of his peers and embarrassed because of his lack of math knowledge. The teacher never asked him to stay after school, never offered to work with him. Never took extra time for him. As one of the assistant football coaches, he had to take off for football practice immediately after school. He didn't have the time to even investigate what the problem might have been with this young man.

And so Batches received a C in freshmen math. He was still eligible to play football.

* * * *

And Batches loved football. This was where this bright, frustrated young man vented his anger. I thank the Lord for his ability in athletics. I don't know what would have become of him if this had not been the case. Batches was big - 6'2", all muscle, strong. He lifted weights.

For many years after Batches left school, I was afraid. I knew the anger in this young man. I was afraid that he might explode at any time. I was afraid that someone in a bar some night, or some time, some place, would call him "stupid" just one more time and he'd kill them.

However, in high school, Batches had the football field on which to vent his anger and frustration. He was a really good player. He had terrific peripheral vision, could see the whole field. This is one of his benefits. The brain is funny that way, when it doesn't give you one skill, it gives you something else. Many people with Batches' characteristics have fantastic peripheral vision.

There were still problems for which Batches had to compensate. He had to check when they called plays to be sure he knew which direction he was to go. He would look down at the scar on his wrist, from his broken arm. If the play went to the left, he would go in the direction of his scar. If the play went to the right, he would go in the opposite direction of his scar.

Batches played defensive end or linebacker. The harder he hit them the better he felt. I remember the time he came home from football practice. "You will never guess what happened today, Mom," Batches said with a grin. "What happened?" I asked.

"Well, our good half back was running full tilt down the field straight at me, and just as I was getting set to stop him, the coach came running at me yelling, 'No Batches, no. Don't hit him.' Boy, mom, I had a good open field shot at him, and the coach wouldn't let me hit him. He was afraid I would hurt him."

Unfortunately, one night during a game a halfback on the opposing team caught the punt and decided to run through the position where Batches was. Batches hit him with a clean cross-chest tackle that laid him right on the sod. You could hear the impact in the bleachers. He didn't get up. I quietly prayed, "Please God, don't let him have hurt that other young man." They brought the ambulance on the field. They put the young man on the stretcher and drove off. Later we learned that he had a broken rib, I was thankful it wasn't more serious.

After the game, we went home where his father confronted Batches. He told him, "I think you should give up football. You are too aggressive and might really hurt someone out there." Batches reacted. He picked up a kitchen chair and threw it at his father.

Batches was angry that his father put his energy into Batches' older brother. His father enjoyed the rewards of watching his oldest son succeed. He withdrew from the reality and pain of watching Batches struggle. I think Batches felt unloved and unlovable. He felt his father didn't understand or care about him. His lack of a relationship with his father has had a tremendous impact on his life.

* * * *

I had a decision to make about Batches and his football career. Batches hurt his back during his Sophomore year. I took him to the doctor and the x-ray showed there was a complication in one of Batches' vertebra. If Batches were to be hit in a certain manner, it might cause terrible impairment. What do I do? Do I take away the only success that this young man has? Do I cross my fingers and pray that no one hits him and causes more damage or possibly cripples him? Do I say "Batches you can't play football anymore?" Could I take away my son's only success?

My decision was to keep quiet and let him play. I left it up to the good Lord. Batches played all through high school without injury.

I know to this day, that had I removed the success that Batches achieved on the playing field, he could possibly have ended his life in an entirely different manner. If he had not been able to have seen some success and some acceptance during his high school days, he might have ended up in prison. There are many unbearable things which a mother can imagine.

* * * *

There were also times he came home from football practice hanging his head. One night he was especially upset. It seems that during practice Batches had been standing on the side lines wearing his helmet. Someone standing behind him didn't realize Batches was there and Batches heard him say, "Boy, that Batches would be a great football player if he weren't so dumb." It was confusing for people - Batches' apparent dumbness and his very real intelligence.

Batches was also the football teams spark plug. I remember one game when Batches didn't play the entire first half. At practice he hadn't played his position. He had been all over the field tackling players and the coach benched him.

His team was losing the game, and I thought the coach might relent and start him after half time. On the first play of the second half, the other team again, ran right through what was usually Batches' position. His coach finally put him in the game. His team mates welcomed him boisterously. They all liked him. His fellow teammates had given him the nickname of 'wild man' because of his tackling ability and hard play. They had practiced against him, knew how hard he hit and how good he was. The team was flat without him. When 'wild man' was finally allowed to participate in the game, the team turned their play around and won the game.

* * * *

28

I remember Batches coming home at dinner time one night and telling us that his art teacher had given him a written test in class that day. Of course, he had turned in his paper with nothing written on it. His art teacher said, "That's okay Batches, I understand." She did not understand. No teacher, during all his years of schooling, ever took the time to find out why this intelligent kid could not learn to read and write. Maybe it was because they had seen those horrible words, "slightly mentally retarded" on his school file and decided any effort on their part would be useless.

* * * *

It was graduation night, 1971. Batches was graduating from high school. All the parents were there, the families, relatives from out of town. We all sat in the bleachers next to the football field. The graduates sat in folding chairs on the field, approximately 150 of them. In front of them was a platform where the principal, assistant principals and members of the Board of Education sat. One microphone stood at the front. Everyone gave their speeches, and each graduate was called by name and made their way up to the platform to receive their diploma.

Time passed, our son was one of the last. Batches made his way to the platform wearing the traditional blue cap and gown. He accepted his diploma, knew by the feel he had really received one, shook hands with the presenter and turned toward the microphone. Holding the diploma above his head, he yelled into the microphone, "ALRIGHT," and proceeded to turn a cartwheel on the stage. Every student clapped. Some parents clapped, some didn't.

I knew why he'd done it. It was an in-your-face gesture, for everything he had had to endure the last thirteen years of his life. I had been alerted earlier that there was a bet with his friend, five dollars, that Batches wouldn't do the cartwheel he told his friend he was going to do.

The following week, an editorial appeared in our city newspaper. A mother that had attended the graduation had written it. She wrote that it was a disgrace that a student from this fine community and school system would turn a cartwheel at the graduation services. She felt the young man should have been penalized for his behavior.

I wanted to write a rebuttal to what she had written. Defend my son's behavior. But I didn't. I didn't want to embarrass Batches again. He'd had enough of that already. I told myself that the important people know the truth. The rest didn't matter.

Batches had his high school diploma; however, it was not worth the paper on which it was written. The teachers read "mentally retarded" on this young man's record, so they wrote him off. Keep him eligible for football, maybe he'll get a football scholarship. A college might not expect him to know how to read. He hadn't been a conduct disorder problem. He sat quietly in class and tried to learn all he could, in spite of his inability to take notes in class.

* * * *

Forty years ago, American education bought Freud's ideas with a vengeance. If children fail, it is caused by their home life or emotional problems. Thus children, with the same problem as Batches, have been told by teachers they could do the work if they just tried harder. They try and try.

But fail. It is not that they are not trying hard enough. The problem is, they are not being taught by the method that would allow them to be successful learners.

CHAPTER 5

Batches received a scholarship to play football at a small college. I guess when you send a young man to college who is functionally illiterate, you're setting yourself up for failure. He made the first string of the football team, but flunked right out of school. There was no way he was equipped to attend college.

There are many athletes today that go to colleges and have four great years of athletics. Yet these athletes are still functionally illiterate when they leave college.

At the time of this writing, many great athletes are coming out of the closet and declaring what their problems have been. At the time Batches went to school, this was a deep-seated secret. If you didn't know how to read, you kept your mouth shut. You didn't tell anyone, that you didn't know how to read.

* * * *

After leaving college Batches went from job to job. He worked construction, worked in a restaurant. However there was one bright spot. Batches had a really good high school friend Bill, whom I love dearly. Bill would say, "Batches how on earth can you beat me all the time in chess and not learn how to read?" Bill, being a very bright student, took it upon himself to make Batches orally learn a word and what it meant, one word every week. Bill didn't realize it, but he was helping Batches tremendously because orally, Batches remembered and knew words. When you talked with Batches, you didn't know anything was wrong. The minute you asked him to put it on paper or to read it, nothing came out right. Bill cared. He couldn't understand why his intelligent friend couldn't read.

Batches was between jobs when he and Bill took off for Florida. One night while they were out at a bar, a gentlemen came up to Batches and said, "How would you like to be a stand-in for George C. Scott in a movie we're making over in the Bahamas? You're his size, his color. Would you consider doing that? If you want to, be at (the airport) tomorrow and we'll fly you over and you can be a stand in." Batches was at that airport the next day.

Batches loved every minute on the set of that movie. He is very artistic. He loved watching all the people, how they handled the lighting. In fact, when he watches films today, he'll say, "See, there's the tracks of the camera, Mom," or "This is an old-time western and there's a modern light pole back there."

Batches lived with Mr. Scott's chauffeur in a motel. One day, when Batches couldn't make change for a dollar, the chauffeur said, "How did you get through high school? You can't even make change for one dollar?" Batches replied, "By playing football."

I'm going to now indulge in a little motherly pride. Here was Batches on the set of a Mike Nichols movie. He was good looking with a lot of personality. Orally, you would have a hard time guessing there was anything wrong because Batches spoke well when not under stress. So one day, the people on the set decided they wanted to take a screen test of Batches; they gave him a script to read. You can guess what happened. By now, you don't really need to guess what happened. You know. He couldn't read it. Another opportunity lost.

* * * *

Batches returned home after the movie was completed. Re-entering the country again, at a Florida airport, he went through U.S. customs. As the customs agent talked with Batches, Batches blocked. He could not process the words he needed to use to answer the agents' questions. It appeared to be suspicious behavior to the agent. Batches had stuffed everything he owned in one back-pack for traveling. The agent grabbed it as it came past him on the revolving belt at the luggage pick up. As the agent removed each item from the pack he threw it back onto the revolving belt. Satisfied that nothing was being smuggled into the country illegally, the agent left Batches to retrieve his belongings as they passed him on the revolving belt. Another embarrassing, humiliating scene. Standing in an airport, in front of a group of strangers, frustrated, picking up and repacking all his personal belongings as they revolved by. Here comes a shoe, here comes a pair of pants, here comes a dirty shirt. Here comes his shaving equipment. Another traumatic experience, time after time after time.

* * * *

Batches stayed home only a short time. He wanted to be on his own. He didn't want to remain a responsibility to his family. He wouldn't admit that he didn't have the skills to make it. Batches went off to Minneapolis with Bill. He was twenty two years old. I wasn't fearful about his decision because he was with Bill. He was given a job of handing out towels in a YMCA. After trying to survive on minimum wage, and sitting there handing out towels, he decided this was not what he wanted to do the rest of his life. Batches left Minneapolis alone. Bill stayed. He had a good job.

I thought my son was still in Minneapolis. Then my oldest son called me from the West Coast, and during our conversation said Batches had stopped by to see him. I said a lot of prayers day and night. I didn't know where he was or what he was doing. He never called. I didn't hear from him for over a year.

As a mother you always say to yourself, "He's going to be alright." Any other thought is too horrible to contemplate. You don't dare dwell on the fact that he might not be alright. So I kept thinking to myself, 'He's a big kid. He's strong. He's street smart. He's a survivor.' I always felt he was a survivor because he had already survived so much. He'd always thought his way out of any trouble he had to face. When he returned, and told me his stories, I found this was true. He had worked his way out of several rather serious incidents.

Batches wandered the country, from town to town for over a year. He hitch-hiked from place to place with his back-pack and pup tent. While he was in Texas, a young black man picked him up to give him a ride. They had just about reached the border of New Mexico when they were stopped by a Texas highway patrolman. The patrolman came up to the car and told Batches to get out of the car. "What are you doing in this car? What are you two up to?" the patrolman asked. "Spread eagle." Batches didn't know what was happening. As far as he knew, they hadn't broken any laws. The patrolman went back to check out their identification. When he came back he informed Batches, "You aren't to be riding with this black man." It was an eye opening experience for Batches. He had never dealt with another person's discrimination before, only his own. Batches ended up walking almost all the width of New Mexico, before he could hitch another ride.

Batches ran out of money. He carried his back-pack, tented in his pup tent, and ate out of garbage pails. He looked for work, all the while walking, hitching rides, going from place to place. One man who picked Batches up begged him to have a sexual relationship with him. Batches told him if he didn't stop the car and let him out, he would kill him. So the man stopped, Batches got out and was so upset he became sick to his stomach right there by the side of the road.

Batches was going through Bakersfield and stopped at a McDonalds, the only restaurant he could afford. It was also the only menu he had memorized, so he didn't have to read it. He set his back-pack down and went to the counter to get his order. When he turned around, his pack was gone. No one he asked had seen anything happen. Included with the only possessions he had, was a beautiful silver dolphin that he had been given by Mike Nichols when in the Bahamas. His extra money, his identification, his clothes, his tent, gone. He had heard that they were hiring people on the docks in Houston, so he headed there. He stayed at Salvation Army Missions along the way.

After Batches arrived in Houston, the people at the employment office were very helpful; they filled out the employment forms for Batches. He went to the dock, but by this time, he was so stressed and had such a poor self image that they didn't hire him.

Around Easter of that year Batches took to the road again, in summer clothes that had been given to him at the Mission. He hitched a ride with a trucker, all the way to

Kentucky. It was spring time, but it turned cold at night. It was late at night when the trucker let him out. At night it is hard to catch a ride, so he walked to get warm. After a while, he realized that the underpass cement had been warmed by the sun during the day. So he crawled up on the warm cement and slept, until he got cold again, and then he'd walk again to the next underpass. He'd climb up there, get a little more warmth, a little more sleep, then walk on. The next day he was picked up by a trucker and driven to within two miles of our home.

After he arrived he told me, "Mom when I walked into The Mission (in Houston) the first time, I could hardly stand the smell of the place. Instead of going to religious services every night, they ought to make those people clean themselves up. Clean up the place. Clean up their clothes. Teach them some life skills. When I walked into the Mission last week and couldn't smell the place anymore, I knew I was in trouble. I had to get out of there."

* * * *

When Batches came back from Texas, he said, "Mom, I need to know how to tell time. I need to know how to make change." I said, "Okay Batches, lets give it a try." Unknowingly, or because someone was looking out for me, I taught him how to make change, and how to tell time, in the way that he could learn. We sat on the floor facing each other. I had accumulated a great deal of different varieties of coins and bills. I said, "Alright, now we're going to play store. I'm going to buy something from you, and I'm going to give you money, and you're going to give me change. You're going to count it back and give me the correct change."

Then he would buy something from me, and I would give him the correct change. This went on for a couple hours that night. A couple hours the next night. A couple hours the next night. I did not realize it at the time, but the touch of the money and the sound of actually speaking, "I need to give you this much money in change. You have paid me this amount, and I need to give you this amount back in change." Counting out loud. Batches was touching the money, moving it back and forth. This sound, touch and motion was exactly the reinforcement that he needed to learn.

To teach Batches to tell time, I started with a child's moveable clock. When the big hand moved the little one also moved. He first learned where the hands should be for all the hours, both a.m. and p.m. There was much repetition, movement, and orally repeating the hour. When he knew these backwards and forwards, I taught him the increments of 5, 10, 15....45, 50 and 55 after the hour. Again, there was practice, saying what the time was, moving the hands to another time, and repeating what time that was. When he had mastered this, he learned the 25, 20, 15, 10 and 5 minutes until the hour in the same manner. Finally, we discussed the minute intervals such as 12 and 24 minutes after and before the hour. There was much motion, sound, touch and repetition. I moved from the simple to the complex, not realizing at the time, this enabled Batches to learn.

* * * *

Batches stayed at home for a while. He looked for work. A neighbor who owned a local bar/restaurant was kind enough to give Batches a job in the kitchen. He moved out of our home and lived in a house near the campus with several college students. After a couple of years, the owner of the bar expanded and opened an identical type place in Arizona. The local manager was being put in charge of the new place, in Arizona. This manager asked if Batches would come out and work for him in Arizona as maintenance man.

So off Batches went to Arizona, with much trepidation on my part. He helped open the restaurant and stayed on as maintenance man. His father and I went out to visit him and he seemed alright. Then after four years of cleaning up vomit and graffiti on the walls, he became unhappy. He became stressed. He didn't like his job and was very upset. He began hearing voices, or so he thought. Stress was doing funny things to him and he realized immediately he needed help. He asked a friend that he worked out with, at the local health club, to go with him to the emergency room.

Why did he need this friend to go with him? Because if you haven't been taught to spell, you can't write, and when you can't write, you can't fill out the forms they give you at the hospital. Telling the doctor what was happening was the easy part. The doctor told him he had done the smart thing to come in to get help, as his stress level was very high. The doctor gave him some medication to relieve his stress and then sent him home.

Batches was questioning, "Where is my life going?" "What am I doing?" "Am I going to be just a janitor all my life?" Batches loves the outdoors. He took long walks up in the mountains in Tucson. Batches and his friends, college students at the University of Arizona, who worked at the bar with him, made trips to San Diego, Mexico, and Las Vegas.

Batches really liked one of the girls in his group of friends, but she was a college student, and he was functionally illiterate. He didn't feel he could be important to her as just a janitor. He found out later that she asked his friend about him quite often, after he left Arizona.

The restaurant that Batches worked at was sold to another group of businessmen. It was a time when the drinking age was raised from eighteen to twenty one. Since this bar/restaurant was located in an area close to a university, the clientele had consisted mainly of students. Income dropped when the age limit went up. The new business owners found that the place was not a financial asset. So the place mysteriously burned to the ground. Not the first time it caught on fire, but the second.

Batches applied for unemployment benefits. However, he still had difficulty explaining his situation to strangers. He sold his clothes, he sold his stereo and other things he had purchased while he had worked the last four years to pay his rent and have time to look for work. One month, he phoned home asking me for money for rent. I sent it to him.

Around this time the woman I worked for retired, and my position was phased out. I also was now unemployed. I guess this was God's way of getting Batches back to his home state. I had been praying all these years for a miracle. A miracle that would help this son of mine learn, what I knew he was intellectually capable of learning.

CHAPTER 6

Batches' father belonged to the Kiwanis club in the city where we lived. The director of a learning center came and gave a talk about children who learn differently. She spoke about children who were bright, children who could not learn language the way in which the schools were teaching it. His father brought home the information that had been given out that day, and said, "I think maybe this person knows what Batches' problem might be." I sat at the kitchen table and picking up the information, began to read.

God provided my miracle. Suddenly, the information that Batches' father had brought home made all the sense in the world. There in my hand, I held the answers I'd been looking for, all those years. In black and white it described the problem that my son had.

It's called dyslexia. I know what the word dyslexia brings to mind, 'a person who reads and writes letters backwards.' Dyslexia is much more than that. I know some educators call it a myth. It's not. You can't live with a myth for twenty years!

I learned there is no one dyslexic exactly like another. Some dyslexics have visual processing problems, some have auditory processing problems. There are dyslexics who are very mildly affected and ones who are severe. If a child has strong auditory skills, then a teacher needs to use auditory skills to teach language. If a child is strong visually, then a teacher must use that visual strength to teach language. It takes a highly qualified language evaluator to determine wherein the strengths and weaknesses of each dyslexic lie.

There on the paper I held, was the dictionary's definition of dyslexia; "dys meaning difficulty, lexia meaning language." Difficulty with language. The international definition of a dyslexic "One who has average, or above average intelligence, has had adequate opportunity to learn language, but has failed to learn language skills, on the level commensurate with their intelligence." There also were the signs and characteristics which I had seen in Batches these many years.

The next month when Batches called me again for rent money, I didn't have any to send him. He replied, "That's okay Mom, I'll make out. I know all the drug dealers in town. We always had to go get drugs for the groups that came in to play at the bar. I'll survive, don't worry about me." I immediately said, "No, you can't do that Batches. No way. Come home. I have found a place. A Center that I know will be able to teach you to read. Please don't get involved with drugs. You couldn't stand it, you're too decent a person. You'd want out and then they'd kill you. It would kill you to sell drugs to children. I know you. Please Batches, please come home. I will help you all I can to go to this Center and learn what I know you can learn."

I spent an awful next ten days wondering, 'Would he really come home?' I'd never lied to him. Would he really believe what I had told him? Please Lord, please bring him back. I just knew, my mother's instinct told me, that this was it. The information said they could teach Batches to read. 'Please Lord, please bring my son back. Help him to come back and learn what I know he can learn.'

Time seemed to drag. I wasn't working but was looking for a job. I'd leave home for a while and wonder, as I was driving back home, if Batches would be there when I got there. One afternoon there was a knock on the door. There stood Batches. I gave him a big hug. I saw the strain on his face. It shouted, 'Thirty years old, here I am, unemployed, defeated, scared, desperate, coming back home to my mom, to help me out one more time. One more failure. What if this doesn't work? What do I do then?'

Batches had come home once more. He'd come back to Mom, not wanting to come, but I had offered him hope. I had offered him another option, and he was willing to give it a try.

As we sat together and talked that day, I could see the lines of stress in his face. Where was the buoyant, inquisitive little boy who had started school all those years ago? What had happened to this stressed-out young man? With eyes downcast, hating himself, no self-esteem of any kind. His self-image had been destroyed.

'Oh Lord, please help me, we have a lot of work to do with this young man. My son has an awful lot of work to do,' I prayed silently as we sat together.

I changed the subject and asked him about his trip. I asked him how he had money enough to get gas to get home. He said, "I charged it on my credit card, Mom. If I only charged five dollars, they wouldn't check to see if the card was overdrawn. I just stopped a lot to buy gas." "That must have seemed forever to come that far and stop at so many gas stations," I replied. He said, "Yeah, it took a lot of time, but I slept in the truck at night, and I didn't need much food. I was just in a hurry to get back." "Are you hungry?" I asked, "Would you like something to eat?" "It would taste pretty good," he said. So I fixed him a sandwich, a glass of milk and I happened to have some ice cream in the refrigerator and a couple of cookies. After he ate, he told me more about his trip home. I tried to focus on the positive. He enjoyed his trip home, seeing this great country of ours. Pondering, I'm sure, what he would find once he got home.

The next morning, I immediately called the Center that had put out the information that I had read and made an appointment for Batches to have an evaluation. He was able to get an appointment in two weeks. In the meantime, Batches got his things together in his room. He didn't have much.

I began to see some of the problems he had after he lost his job in Tucson. Where was his stereo, his gorgeous western boots, his good clothes we had seen when we were in Tucson? He had sold them to buy food. He had bought a twenty-five pound sack of potatoes and ate them for a month for food. He doesn't like potatoes to this day. He had difficulty filling out job application forms. He had lost his self esteem. His hang dog appearance made employers leery of hiring him. He even had gone to an audition for a modeling job. They liked his walk and his look, but when they gave him an ad to read, you can guess the rest.

Shortly after Batches returned home his truck was repossessed. His dad made the statement to him that he was stupid for not informing the bank of his situation. Before I could blink my eyes, Batches had his dad on the floor hitting him. I pulled him off as quickly as I could. Batches turned and went to his room. I quietly told his father he was never to use the word stupid with his son ever again. I think Batches' reaction caused him to realize that anger and frustration had built up in his son. He has never again used the word stupid. I paid off the twelve hundred dollar balance on his truck, plus the cost to the local dealer who had taken it. Another blow to Batches' self esteem.

* * * *

44

Batches went out to the Center on his own. He worked with the evaluator all morning taking a series of tests. During the evaluation, Batches felt very vulnerable, very exposed, letting another person see the extent of his illiteracy. They made no comment about what they thought, just told him to come back in a week for the results of the evaluation.

In the interim, Batches, with my help, wrote to Caro State Hospital where he had been tested in the second grade. He requested a copy of his report. It came in the mail before he had his next appointment at the Center.

I was furious when I opened that letter and read that report. All of a sudden, everything about school and how Batches had been treated fell into place. There was this terrible conclusion at the very end of the report saying, "This boy presents evidence of mental retardation." Because he read two years below grade level, they labeled him slightly mentally retarded. Oh, how I wish I had known that was on Batches' record. Suddenly, I realized why his sixth grade teacher had said to me, "Please have that son of yours retested. He is doing things that he should not be able to do." I would have had him retested instead of asking the opinion of a psychologist, who had limited contact with my son. I would have found a way to pay for it. I could kick myself many, many times over, because perhaps at that point, maybe I could have found someone who recognized his problem. We would not have waited all these years to find out what Batches' real problem was.

Batches' anger grew, as I read him the report. "Those sons of bitches didn't know what they were seeing. They thought they had to make a decision, so they said mentally retarded. They never learned anything in college, about people like me. They made a wrong decision that ruined my life, and they are still holding jobs, still doing this to others because they don't research all possible areas of inability to read. Why couldn't they just have said they didn't know what they were seeing? They didn't want to look stupid, but they caused everyone in school to call me stupid, ignorant and retard!"

With trepidation and fear, Batches, his father and I went back to the Center to find out the results of his evaluation. The evaluator at the Center was not optimistic. Batches' skill level was so low, they had trouble evaluating him. His overall language skill level, they told us, was third grade; however, his oral language was excellent. I thought his reading had to be a little higher than third grade level, because he had survived all those years.

The good news was they were willing to tutor him for a period of three months. If they found that he was capable of learning to read with the method by which they taught, they would continue to tutor him.

CHAPTER 7

Batches started on his way. The tutor mentioned the importance of practicing what he learned, between lessons. Lessons were set up twice a week. An hour and one-half each lesson, because they felt his concentration level was excellent. He could accept instruction for that length of time. He worked hard.

Batches would go down to the basement when he got tired of studying and punch at his bag. He'd bought a punching bag and gloves. I know this helped alleviate the stress of all the work he was doing. Persons like Batches can work only so long. Then, because they are expending so much more energy to learn, they need recreational breaks. They need to stop their lessons, and for fifteen minutes jog, bike, anything active, to break the tension of learning. The involvement of motion on the punching bag with the saying of sounds and syllables also helped him to learn his language skills.

Batches worked with motion and touch and sound. Motion, touch, sound; over and over. He worked with the sounds of the letters. He worked with the blending of sounds to make syllables, and then put the syllables together, to make a word. He put the words together to read. He also worked on comprehension, to understand what he was reading. All the time he was improving immensely.

I bought Batches a tape recorder and tapes, something he should have had and been able to use in high school. Batches taped his lessons. He worked very hard on those lessons between tutoring sessions. He would listen to those tapes over and over.

At the end of three months the Center found out Batches was really learning. He was doing well. He loved it. His self-esteem wasn't as close to the floor as it had been. It was a tremendous relief for Batches, to finally know that he wasn't mentally retarded, he was dyslexic.

The Center retested him after nine months. They felt he had made tremendous progress, and they wanted to find out exactly how much. The retest showed that Batches, in nine months time, had gone from a reading skill level of third grade to a senior in high school level. This learning had taken place, because Batches was being taught language in the way in which he could learn!

As Batches and I returned home after his re-evaluation, Batches said, "Do you realize that the schools wasted ten years of my life?" What a profound statement. Unfortunately, there are other children whose lives are being wasted because they are not being taught to read in the way in which they can learn. Unfortunately, there are numerous adults whose school lives were wasted.

Batches had reached a senior in high school reading level, but he is still dyslexic. It doesn't go away. He still needs extra time to process language. He still needs to work very hard to accomplish his goals.

Batches' college tutor used a story he wrote for a report she did. The following are part of her report and Batches' story (Dr. Alice L. Hamachek, Professor, Dept. of Education, Central Michigan University):

I am enclosing in this report a creative story written by a dyslexic learner. The final copy of the story will never show the hours of agonizing energy that were expended to produce it, but it will show the dedication, the persistence and the creative skill that dyslexic persons seem to possess.

"The Red House on the Hill" is a story which symbolizes the battered emotions of the person who attempts to withstand the years of struggle against the forces that are constantly threatening defeat. Day after day, the dyslexic learner is placed in a school environment and asked, directly or indirectly, to think like everyone else, to learn like everyone else and to produce academically like everyone else. Yet the dyslexic knows that is impossible, because the "thinking mechanism" isn't designed the same way. Still, in a desperate attempt to meet up to expectations, the dyslexic keeps on trying. The end results, however, in the majority of situations, is failure. Failure, not because the student hasn't tried, but because it was an impossible task.

This story is more than a creative story, it is a reflection of the defiance and the desperate struggle to succeed and feel like a worthwhile member of the human race. It is an expression of the determination to not give up. It is my hope that as educators we will strive to understand the dyslexic learner and make every effort to appreciate the potential of each mind that we teach.

The Red House on the Hill

The old faded red house on the steep rocky hillside was slowly falling apart from the elements. And on this cold rainy tempest night, there was no exception. The tempest was trying its best to tear down that reluctant stubborn house with every vicious, depraved gust of wind it could hurl at that old, but proud, red faded house on the hill.

The demonic tempest grew more enraged by this red faded old house. Why should this house stand up against him! How dare that rotten piece of junk of a house stand up against my powerful gusts of wind and my driving rain? Newer houses before had bowed down before me or they simply blew apart.

Then with a treacherous snicker, the tempest said, as he started to increase in size, "We shall see how you stand up against this, you decrepit antique of a house!" The tempest was gathering wind and rain, like an out-of-control vacuum cleaner sweeping the skies and bellowing as it grew and bulged into a humongous size. Then, crouching low near the little red house, the tempest unleashed his wrath full force on the frightened little house.

The wind and rain came with more intensity this time. Like a jet racing across the sky, the wind and rain hit the faded red house on the hill full strength. The tempest was making it twist and bend and shake!

The old oak wood planks on the red faded house were painfully crying out as they creaked and moaned while the beastly tempest pounded it with wind and rain. Then suddenly, from deep within the house, came yells of defiance. You bloody bag of wind! You rotten blackguard! But the cries of defiance were muffled by the sounds of splintering wood and cries of pain.

The tempest had succeeded in tearing off three rotten loose oak planks from the corner of the right side. The old faded red house literally clung for its very life to the rocky wet hillside. But, the will to survive was strong inside the old red faded house as the tempest battered and bruised its timbers. It did not come apart, and so the inner survival spirit grew stronger every minute as the tempest started to weaken in power.

The infuriated rapscallion tempest knew and could feel its strength being drained little by little as the first warm soft dawning rays of sunlight broke ever so gently through some enormous black thunder clouds.

The crisp clear azure sky and the warm southern air drifted unhurriedly up from the south while the sun slowly rose majestically behind the red faded old house. The sun and its two companions had already begun to drain the life and strength out of the tempest. But, before they could, the tempest was off like a deer, darting and dancing and screaming "I will be back! I will be back you inept incipient pile of retarded rotten wood." Then he went off searching to harass or to beat on or to destroy another one of his victims. He was a nonstop demon!!

YES! The tempest had decamped! Breathing a sigh of relief, the little red faded old house leaned back and took in the new morning rays of the sun and the fresh clean air of the "after storm" The rays warmed his weary beaten frame and the clean fresh air filled him with a new hope. He had survived the ordeal once more! His eye caught the glimmer of a faint distant rainbow, but the haunting words of "I will be back" echoed through his wooden frame. "Yes, he will be back, but I will be here!"

Turning once more to see if the faint glimmer of the Iris was still there, he softly paused and said, "I will be here, I will be here!!"

* * * *

Our family didn't have much money at the time Batches was being tutored at the Center. I still was not working full-time. What jobs I had paid five dollars per hour.

And here came the bills for dictionaries and books. Batches would go downtown and bring back a book. He'd go again the next week and bring back another book. He could not absorb what he was learning fast enough. I could not tell him that I couldn't afford for him to buy all these books, so we made do.

Shortly after Batches reached a senior in high school reading level, he got a job as a maintenance person with a local school. This took some of the financial burden off me. Batches was now able to pay for his own lessons. The rehabilitation services for our State stopped paying for his lessons when he reached a senior high level in reading. According to their policy, he was capable of going out and getting a job, but Batches had no intention of quitting. He wasn't satisfied. He wanted to read at college level.

Batches accomplished college level in a very short time. Our local community college did not require the ACT test if one were a citizen of the county, so with trepidation, Batches went to enroll in a single class.

The first day that Batches went back into a classroom, after all those years, he had a panic attack, but he hung on. He said, "Mom, I wanted to toss my cookies, I wanted to run. The palms of my hands were perspiring. I wanted to get out of there. All the old feelings from before came pounding down on my head and on my chest. I felt like I had an iron weight sitting right on my chest, but I fought it off, Mom. I fought it off and I stayed."

Batches' next panic attack came at his first mid-term. He again had all the symptoms of the day when he had first walked into the classroom at the college. He wanted to run again. He wanted to get out of there. He began questioning himself, 'Can I do a test? Oh geeze, a test.' Batches had been told, when he registered at the handicap office, that he would have all the time that he needed to take his tests. The professor teaching the class had agreed, but Batches still doubted himself. Even after all he had learned, would he be able to pass a college test?

When Batches' test came back, he'd gotten a C on his mid-term. It was hard work and a lot of studying, but Batches passed that first class as a freshmen in college with a C. What a triumph for him!

* * * *

Fifteen years after graduation from high school, Batches taught himself the math tables. He was able to do this because he could now read the instructions. He went on to pass his college algebra class. His professor gave him a C - average work, right? RIGHT. This time the C was deserved. Batches did learn.

* * * *

When Batches signed up for his first English class at the Community College, he was told he would be required to take a spelling test. His heart dropped as he learned this, especially when he was told he would not be allowed extra time to take this test. Of course he failed it and was informed he would have to take remedial reading. However, Batches also registered for the English class he wanted to take. One of his instructors had told him they could not keep him out of a class if he wished to take it.

Upon arriving at his remedial class, he discussed his dyslexia thoroughly with his remedial teacher. She had never heard of it! I could not believe that a remedial language professor in a community college had never heard about dyslexia. She really didn't know quite what to do with him and suggested a vocabulary test. Batches took this test, untimed, and reached a fourteenth grade level in vocabulary. The teacher looked at this and said, "Batches, you obviously know what you need. You make up your own curriculum for this remedial class." He spent time in the lab two days a week to improve his reading speed.

His ability to have a high level of vocabulary was the fact that he had studied the book Instant Vocabulary, by Ida Erlich, Pocket Books, Simon and Schuster, New York, New York, April, 1979. This contains prefixes, roots and suffixes. He had learned this book backwards and forwards. Thus, even though he came across a word for which he did not know the meaning, he could figure it out, from the meaning of the prefix, root and suffix.

Even after dyslexics finish their education and get a job, they are still dyslexic and need time to process language in their unique style.

* * * *

After three terms of working forty hours a week as a maintenance person and taking one class each term, Batches came to me and said, "Mom, you know how old I am. If I continue working and taking one class a term, I'm going to be fifty before I get my college degree." I replied, "Do you feel that you could handle at least two classes now?" Batches said, "Yes, I feel that I probably could take not a full load, not fifteen hours - but, perhaps eleven hours. I could take two classes plus another that is not difficult and really begin to get my college education."

A wonderful man in our church congregation approached Batches at a rare time when he went to church with me. He told Batches about an excellent field of study. This man knew about Batches' interest in the outdoors, in camping, in canoeing, in hiking, so he suggested to him that he go to a university about eighty miles from our home and talk to the Therapeutic Recreation Department. He felt Batches would be very successful in this profession.

Batches made a visit to that university, and he came home with an excellent idea. He had picked up information on the freshmen and sophomore classes that would be required in Therapeutic Recreation. By getting this information from the university, where he would like to transfer, and following their schedule of required courses, transferring was much easier. When Batches applied for a transfer, after his sophomore year, all his classes from the community college transferred. He was able to enter the university as a full-fledged junior.

CHAPTER 8

These were not the easiest times for Batches, not for me and not for his father. It's hard to have a child return, after they have been out on their own, to the home. It's hard to bite your tongue and not ask, 'Where you going? When will you be back? Will you be here for dinner?' It was also hard for Batches to come back and have to say, 'I'll be home for dinner, I'll be back at six.' Batches had been on his own. He had not had to report to anyone.

There were times when I would have liked to watch a television show, but I didn't turn on the television because Batches could not learn if he was distracted. It is a paradox because Batches learns through creating sound and motion, yet to be able to concentrate he cannot have distractions of sound or motion about him.

There was much give and take on the part of both myself and Batches, but we made it work. We had to make it work. This was absolutely his last chance to make something of himself.

* * * *

Reading the morning paper, a name suddenly caught my eye. My throat tightened with fear and disbelief, as I again read the name, age, and family names from the obituary column. Through my tears, I managed to call the Center. Questions flew through my mind. Had they seen it? What had happened? The Center would check on it and call me back.

Turning from the phone I thought of Mike. The articulate, intelligent young man who so often stopped at my desk to chat when he finished his lesson. He had a great sense of humor and loved life. He always left feeling better about himself; the Center was the one place that truly understood him. Mike had come to the Center because he was failing his college classes. His goal was to finish college; however, his family did not understand.

The family had a successful business. Mike had become a partner when his father retired. His brother and sister had given him a job running errands and driving the truck to deliver supplies. They did not understand his need to go to college. After all, he wasn't intelligent enough to pass the classes.

Mike wanted to be more than just a delivery boy. Three times he had left town and gone elsewhere to find another job, only to return again to the family business. This seemed to confirm his family's belief - Mike wasn't intelligent enough to make it on his own. Mike knew his older siblings would never allow him to be more than an errand boy. If only his family had understood, that in spite of his learning differences, Mike could accomplish his goal. Their intelligent brother could be more than an errand boy.

The ringing of the phone interrupted my thoughts. It was the Center. Mike had taken his own life. He had gone to an old office building, owned by the business, where old supplies, furniture, and other office items were placed when they were no longer useful - the discards. How prophetic this act seemed to me. Mike's teachers, his peers, and his family had never understood or accepted him for what he was, a different learner.

Mike must have decided that all options were closed to him, except one. Instead of turning his frustration and anger into a driving force to reach his goal, he turned it on himself. Without his family's support, he couldn't make it. The obituary that Mike's family had written reinforced this, Mike was listed as an employee of the company, not as one of the owners.

* * * *

Batches felt like he was climbing a mountain. He'd come home and tell me, "Mom I've made it a couple of steps higher today." Then, there were the days when he'd come home and say, "I thought I was half-way up my mountain, but I've slipped back to the bottom." He'd start again, to climb his mountain.

Batches was like a chrysalis trying to emerge into a beautiful butterfly. Trying to once again become that wide eyed person, head held high, ready to try his wings, who had so happily skipped off to kindergarten.

Batches wrote of his feelings. He said writing down his feelings on paper was a kind of healing. "Tearing down walls Mom, I'm tearing down walls," he would say, over and over, after he returned home from Arizona. Walls he had built to protect himself from the slurs and slights of his school mates, teachers, adults, strangers who didn't understand what it was like to be dyslexic. People who didn't understand what it was like, to try and try so hard, over and over, and then fail. People had pounded him into someone with absolutely no self esteem.

During remediation he wrote, "I hang on to my past, like a child that hangs on to a book for balance. I must let go and walk, but I am so afraid of falling. I feel like a near miss, when two cars almost hit one another."

During college he wrote, "I worry about failing this test and class. I wish I could climb out of this pool and rest for a moment, so I could catch my breath. Where is the justice or fairness in all this? It feels lopsided to me. I feel like the fat man who is supposed to run six miles, and can only run one. I feel like the weight lifter who can only lift a hundred pounds, and is supposed to lift two hundred pounds."

"Thursday will come and go, and I will remain."

"I am shaking, like when I dance the first dance with Alice. My hands and body are shaking. Must be an anxiety attack. Will I ever get over them? I fight doing school work. Do I want to fail? I must want to."

"The emotion bubbles up from my insides, and it comes out through my eyes in tears. I feel weak and drained of emotion. I think another wave of emotion has hit shore and is running back into the sea. I hope the redecorating is almost finished inside myself. I know I could not go through another complete overhaul of myself again."

"I must relax, and let the wave hit shore and wash away. I think I have a handle on my class in Life Science 123, Thursday will be my big test. I must do well in this class to go on. Am again becoming uncomfortable with myself, must be this test I am going to take Thursday. Can't find myself. Hope it gets better, have tears in my eyes the last two days. Maybe this will pass. Class was interesting. Another wave hit the shore and the sadness is very much in my eyes. Is it because I am dyslexic, or is it because I could be somewhere else, doing something else, if I would have had the training earlier? I think, or I hope I will know this answer down the road. Time is a factor here. So be gentle with yourself, and find the bright side, all is not lost if you do not go on through college. The sun will come up the next day. For every triumph, I have the sadness or pain from the past."

"I do not know the date, but that is not unusual. Feel good about myself today. Did well on living science class test today..... I hope it continues to get better. Don't feel as uptight about myself. Tend to drift back to old ways sometimes. Catch myself looking down, and talking to wall and floor, when I should be looking at the person. Must start using my vocabulary...."

"I feel pain which causes me sorrow, like waves crashing on to shore. I wonder if the storm that is inside me will pass. The feeling of feeling stupid comes and goes. I wonder if this will pass. I know I can not quit, but the urge is great some times. I must find out why. I feel stupid when someone tries to help me read or write. The sadness is leaving, I must do this more often. Writing seems to help. I am still shaky about myself...."

* * * *

A severe classic dyslexic, in order to attempt college work, must have a great deal of support. That is, if they have not been taught appropriately by the schools at a young age. I became Batches' tutor. I became the person who helped fill in the information that he should have learned in public school. Much of his new college material went on from what he had supposedly learned in high school classes. Therefore, I became the teacher. I filled in the missing material that he had not gotten from his high school courses.

When it came to the class on government, I had to teach him about the House of Representatives, the Senate, the Judiciary branch. All the facts he should have learned in high school. I filled in the missing puzzle pieces, so he could pass his college level courses. This is why it is so important for schools to teach these children language skills at the elementary level, so they can learn.

Dyslexics need to be identified in junior high, and high school too, if they "fell through the cracks." They need to be remediated, taught language skills by teachers that have been trained to teach dyslexics.

* * * *

During late summer, my sister and I drove Batches up to the University. My car was loaded down with Batches' personal stuff, just like every other kid going off to college. After unloading his stuff at his dorm, we went to lunch at a local eatery. After lunch we dropped him off, and I watched him walk toward the dorm. A question lingered in the back of my mind, "Without his home support system, would he be able to make it on his own?"

* * * *

I have finally let go of the guilt I carried around with me all these years. I've stopped blaming myself for Batches' dyslexia. Experts believe dyslexia may be caused by naturally occurring brain differences. However, I still carry with me a great deal of anger at the way my son was treated by the public schools. I want children like Batches to be taught how to read and write in our public school systems.

INFORMATIONAL

CHAPTER 9

After Batches started his tutoring at the Center, and I could see the tremendous difference it made, I wanted to learn all I could about dyslexia. I became a volunteer, and then an employee at the Center where Batches was being tutored.

In 1920, Dr. Samuel Orton, a mental health professional, was really concerned over the numbers of intelligent children brought to him because they hadn't learned to read, write and spell. In spite of having the very best teaching being offered, these intelligent children commonly failed to learn. He realized children like Batches were not a rarity.

Dr. Orton had a grant from the Rockefeller foundation to carry on this research. Orton's studies showed that these children's visual perception was normal. He noted the ambidexterity of these children. They could write as well with one hand as the other. And often times, could even write their names upside down. He pointed out the relationship of stuttering to this problem, an often neglected fact. He saw the frequency of left-handedness, in families that showed this problem. There was also a high rate of similar disorders in one family. It seemed possibly to be inherited, genetic, more males than females were affected. However, current data indicates that equal numbers of males and females are affected. Sometimes slowness in learning to speak was present. There could be a degree of clumsiness in these children, but he also noted that sometimes they were excellent athletes with highly developed coordination and awareness of their bodies in space.

Orton pointed out that teaching these children to learn must be through phonics and must be approached from the simple to the complex, in a very structured manner. (Orton-Geschwind, Norman, M.D. Why Orton Was Right. Orton Dyslexia Society, Annal of Dyslexia, Vol. 32, 1982, pp. 2-4.)

In 1946, Anna Gillingham, in her work with Dr. Samuel Orton and others in the language project of the New York Neurological Institute, developed a manual for teaching children like Batches. (Orton, June L. The Orton-Gillingham Approach. Baltimore: The Johns Hopkins Press, 1966, p. 138). "....no other work has had such a monumental influence over the teaching of dyslexic children (as the Orton-Gillingham approach). Subsequent programs and ideas, if they have not grown directly from this initial work, have certainly had to take it into account." (Naidro, S. Teaching Methods and Their Rationale. New York, John Wiley and Sons, Inc., 1981.)

The Orton-Gillingham Kinesthetic Tactile approach, which was used to teach Batches came from what is now the Dyslexia Institute of Minnesota and Reading Center, 847 5th Street Northwest, Rochester, Minnesota, 55901, (507) 288-5271 (www.thereadingcenter.org). The Center, where Batches was tutored originally, sent four people to Minnesota to learn the Orton-Gillingham, Kinesthetic Tactile approach. Over the past twenty years, the approach learned in Minnesota has been modified and improved by the Directors and the tutors at the Center.

Dr. Orton learned that no matter how hard they try, fifteen percent of the population cannot adequately learn language, without direct multisensory structured language education. This holds constant, regardless of the educational fad in use, such as the 'see and say' method, by which Batches was taught. The reason is not because these children have brain damage; it is because their brain functions differently. Therefore they need to learn differently. **Teaching approach needs to match learning style!**

Dr. Larry Silver, an authority concerning problem children, wrote in the 1940's, 'Children with neurologically based learning difficulties were called brain damaged, but they appeared normal. Thus, the term minimal brain damage was used.' Observation and testing of these children showed no evidence of brain damage. Research pointed out that the problem was in how the brain neurologically functioned, not a damaged brain. (Silver, Larry B., M.D. The Misunderstood Child. New York: McGraw-Hill, 1984, p. 17.)

MRI brain scan shows there is a difference in the structure of the brain of a dyslexic. MRI stands for Magnetic Resonance Imaging. So called 'normal' brains show a different MRI scan structure. MRI scans are similar to CAT scans in that a person is placed in a chamber to have the scan done. There the similarity ends. MRI units use powerful electromagnets to line up hydrogen atoms in the brain, a radio frequency generator to knock them out of line, and a computer to detect the signals the atoms emit. The signals are converted into a sharp image on a video screen that indicates the shape and location of various brain structures. (Rickelman, Robert J. and Henk, William A. Reading technology and the brain. The Reading Teacher, January, 1990, p. 334.)

Included in the report I received from Caro State Hospital where Batches was tested was the statement, 'The EEG shows less electrical current in the left-side, in the language area' which supports the fact that Batches is dyslexic. The psychologist and medical personnel at the hospital either had not known about Dr. Orton's research or had written his theories off. I don't know to this day which it was.

* * * *

Dr. Manual Gomez, Head of Pediatric Department, Mayo Clinic, a pediatric neurologist made this statement, "There are more dyslexics needing special teaching techniques than all the blind, deaf and mentally impaired combined."

* * * *

Dyslexia is often called the hidden disability. Many dyslexics keep hidden the problem of their difficulty with language, especially their inability to read. Dyslexics may start to develop 'masks' in the first or second grade to hide the problem. They don't want to be called stupid, dummy, retard. Often, they became the class clown. They crack a joke to distract the teacher and class when they don't know the answer. Cher admits that this is what she did.

Sometimes, the adult dyslexic develops a super-competency 'mask.' "Oh that's easy, sure, anyone would know that," still not giving the answer. Some just sit at the back of the class, hoping the teacher won't notice them. Then secretly try to get classmates to do the work for them.

Some dyslexics try to show their intelligence by being too verbal in class. The teacher wants their response in writing, but they can only give it verbally. Unfortunately, the teacher sees the student as being disruptive in class.

Another 'mask,' "I'm Joe cool. Nobody gets close to me, but I'm a leader because I'm the best jock in school."

Bruce Jenner, Olympic decathlon champion, Greg Loganis, Olympic diver, and Dexter Manly, Washington Redskin's player, all achieved success through their athletic abilities. Another 'mask,' the class bully, "I'll throw this book at you if you mess with me." They would rather be thought of as bad, then dumb. ("Instructor," April, 1989, by permission of Sally L. Smith from American Inquiry Magazine, 1987, by American University, p. 27-32.)

There are many successful people today who are dyslexic. Some have employees who assist with the written skills that they themselves have not acquired. Dyslexics are often excellent artists, musicians, very creative people who can read people's faces well (good salespersons) and are intuitive. These are some of the special gifts given to dyslexics.

Batches had a 'mask.' He was a very good boy who did everything asked of him, made no waves, and sat at the back of the class in silence. Teachers need to be aware of children who are too quiet, too good in class. Anger and frustration often lie beneath the surface.

The schools need to reach these dyslexic children in the early years of their academic career. The schools need to teach them language skills in the way they can learn before they begin to wear these masks, before their mental health is affected. Dyslexics need to be successful at learning so they do not feel powerless. They should be allowed to set goals for themselves and obtain them. Perhaps then they would not feel hopeless. They must be reached before they drop out or are expelled from school, and many of life's doors are closed to them.

* * * *

Our prisons are filled with functionally illiterate men and women. This poem by C.J. Bailey expresses it best.

The Boy

A few years ago my accumulation of experiences allowed me the ability to write and develop a project that worked with the judicial system and I called it "Sentenced to Read." My thoughts have often struggled as to how do I capture this cause which speaks for those kids that don't know how to speak for themselves? The answer, as always: Keep it simple and tell the story.

> *I first saw him that day in a county courtroom.*
> *He was a fair haired boy of fifteen...blond hair*
>   *and blue eyes.*
> *The court docket charge was there to see*
> *A felon in the third degree.*
> *The boy...well, he couldn't read!*
> *No one knew this at the time...*
> *Oh...they all assumed he was just out of line.*
> *The night before he'd robbed a store.*
> *"A felony charge," said the judge...*
> *"Why did you do it?"...echoed through the*
>   *courtroom walls.*
> *Fear gripped this boy of fifteen...*
> *If he could only tell them what was so...*
> *What he'd discovered so long ago...*
> *That booze and pills would ease this pain.*
> *Dare he tell the judge...of his shame?*
> *His memory told him — No!*

His answer was..."I don't know."
Tears fell on the courtroom floor that day...
And as I heard the judge say...
"One year for you...
Maybe you'll discover — Why! You don't know."
Through his eyes I saw...a part of me...
I heard the words of the heart — that went
  unspoken.
This story is true.
The tears that fell were real...!
But the tragedy of all tragedies goes untold.
You see...this blue eyed boy, still can't read!
Was justice done that day?
Some say maybe...some say maybe there will be the
  time...
The courtroom walls will echo this line...
I can't read...Dear God, I can't read...

Epilogue:

Do you see what I see?
Do you hear what I hear?
This has been the boy — we sometimes call
  delinquent — the juvenile.

* * * *

As a parent and as educators, you need to fit the way you teach a child, to the way in which that child can learn. "Dr. Howard Gardner, a psychologist and professor of education at Harvard University, is convinced there are many different kinds of intelligence. In his book, Frames of Mind, the Theory of Multiple Intelligences, Gardner argues that there is no such thing as a single intelligence, measurable by a standard IQ test. He feels the schools only emphasize two of them, linguistic (having the ability to use words effectively) and logical-mathematical (having the ability to reason well). Gardner says, "There's a danger that people will say a child who isn't verbal or mathematical is just stupid." Other intelligences include musical (having a keen ear and sense of rhythm), spatial (having a talent for visual imagery or for appreciating relationships in space), kinesthetic (having grace or agility), and interpersonal (being gifted at understanding others)." (Working Mother, Sept. 1989, pp. 76-78)

Most classrooms today are set-up to teach children who learn in the "standard" way. Most teachers in our public school system themselves, learn in the "standard" way and do not understand students who learn differently. Schools need to implement polices so that each child has an equal chance to succeed at learning. Perhaps if schools allowed curricula that was solid but nontraditional, more creative, diverse people would be drawn to and remain in the honored profession of teaching.

* * * *

The Goals 2000: Educate America Act was passed by the United States Senate on March 26, 1994. Teachers, parents and administrators at each school will design and implement their own reform programs. The people who do well in the school environment, as it is now structured, will be the majority voice heard during reform planning. The focus will be on class content and testing. Students will be tested to find out if they have mastered specific goals. How can dyslexics master goals when they are not being taught in a way they can learn? How can they pass these tests? What will happen to them? Will parents and students continue to take the blame for failure?

It is a national goal or it should be, to educate its citizens. An informed citizenry is a powerful citizenry. Of what are we afraid?

The State of Michigan reports that the cost to support an illiterate individual through her/his lifetime is $500,000.00. If a person can not read well enough to be employed with a job that pays no better than minimum wage, s/he can't pay the rent. How much better to spend these monies to train teachers to teach dyslexics! How much better to spend the money to restructure our educational system so that all students can learn!

CHAPTER 10

Having spoken with many parents in my eight years of work at the Center, I can relate to the frustration, anger and pain I heard in their voices. Their stories were all different, yet painfully similar. They were all looking for answers to the question, "Why can't my intelligent child learn to read?"

The one remark I heard the most on the phone from parents was "The school keeps saying it is developmental." The schools seem to be implying that the children will outgrow their condition. Some had children in the fourth and fifth grades, and the school was still telling them it was developmental. The parents realized how far behind their children were, especially in reading, and were concerned.

What the schools should say is: Dyslexia is developmental which means the brain difference and unique structure is there from birth. The brain as it is uniquely constructed determines how it will learn.

Instead parents turned to the Center for evaluations and help.

* * * *

One morning, an eight year old boy reluctantly followed his mother into the Center. Dragging his feet, he trudged along to the room where he was going to be evaluated. My co-worker smiled at me then shut the door behind him.

After lunch, the boy sat in on the discussion and recommendations of the work he had done in the morning. All at once, the door to the conference room was thrown open. He came tearing out with the biggest smile and wide-eyed said to me, "I found out I'm not dumb, I'm smart, I'm just dyslexic."

* * * *

Many mothers described the same scenario, 'My child is getting A's in math, science, orchestra and art but D's and E's in subjects such as English and History.' When they realized they had finally found someone that understood their child and could speak intelligently with them about their child, they often broke down crying. They were so relieved that they had reached someone who understood their child.

* * * *

Todd, a fourteen year old, came in for his first lesson. He was dressed in black. His head was shaved on one side and his hair was black except for one red streak. A skull hung from his right ear, and distrust shown out of his eyes. He had problems at home and at school. His behavior was very inappropriate, and he was disrespectful toward teachers and his parents. What I discovered was a very angry, very hurt child, behind the facade.

At first, our lessons consisted of Todd's expressing his anger and listening to me read to him. He was very reluctant to read or write, but eventually I convinced him to read a play with me. Finally, he was able to write short stories. His anger at how he had been treated in an unsympathetic school environment, his impression that he is 'stupid' were very evident in the writing.

One day, Todd's mother called to tell me that he would no longer be attending lessons. He had been committed to a psychiatric hospital for evaluation.

* * * *

More than one parent told me they had called to discuss dyslexia with the principal at their child's school. The principal assured the parent that the school's special education teacher could teach dyslexic students. Upon further investigation, this was found to be untrue. The teacher had no specific training in teaching language skills to dyslexics.

One parent told me she had spoken with the junior high school counselor about her dyslexic daughter. The parent told the counselor her daughter needed time to process language. When her daughter was given adequate time to complete a test, she scored two grade levels higher than sixth grade, but when her daughter had to complete a timed test, she scored two grade levels lower than sixth grade. The counselor told her, "It isn't possible for your daughter to be given any more time than the other students in regular classes. She's going to have problems next year here at the junior high." Would the counselor expect an intelligent student in a wheelchair to run the 50 yard dash?

This same parent told me she had also spoken with her child's current teacher. She had told the teacher that her child learned differently and needed more time to complete her work. The teacher told her, "(Your child) needs to realize, that she will have to function like the other children in the real world." In fact, approaching the teacher only brought out his hostility. Two days later, her child begged her mother not to talk to her teacher anymore.

Many teachers do not understand why an intelligent student will not do his/her homework like the other children. They tell parents, "They could do it if they wanted to. They just don't want to." These teachers use punishments to try to make the student like the other children. "No recess, no joining in with the other kids for fun activities if you won't do your work like the other children." Many parents are choosing to home school their children because of these and other problems with the public school system. These children are so misunderstood by society and our educational system.

* * * *

Joe had been a mason in the construction industry for many years. He was also a non-reader. He looked at the pictures on the blue-prints to accomplish his work. Joe's main problem was finding his way to work when the job locations changed. He could not read street-signs. His wife had to drive him to work for the first two or three days until he learned the way.

Joe heard about the Center when he was 48 years old. He made the decision that he would try once more to learn to read, so he could read his Bible. His family were all college graduates and well read. Joe always felt out of place at family gatherings. His poor vocabulary left him unable to comprehend some of the conversation, and he remained quietly in the background.

One day, Joe came for his lesson with a huge smile on his face. In his hand was a small white envelope. He said, "Guess what I did today? Today, for the first time ever, I bought my wife a birthday card! I can read the cards."

* * * *

One phone call I received was from a gentleman who was an inspector on the line at an automobile plant. He was worried because they wanted to promote him to manager of the line, and that meant he had to write reports. He had been doing his present job by having memorized what each number meant. He couldn't read or write.

Many dyslexics, who have excellent hands on capabilities, went to work at the automobile plants in the fifties, sixties and seventies. These people can look at something and build it. They made a good living. However, with the shutting down of many automobile plants in the United States, we hear that these companies are having to retrain their workers, so they can obtain other jobs. Many are dyslexics who fell through the cracks of the Public School System and now realize they must learn to read.

* * * *

Sam, who is in his mid-thirties, has a good job with the Post Office as a mail carrier. He had just recently admitted to his sister that he could not read. He does his job by matching up numbers and street names to the envelopes. When his co-workers pass around sheets with jokes on them, he counts how many seconds it takes them to laugh. Then when he is passed the paper, he counts and laughs at the appropriate time.

Sam hides around corners at work and listens to co-workers discuss memos that are posted. He cannot read them. His sister feels he can learn to read, but he flat out rejects any help. His educational experiences were too traumatic, and he's gotten along so far not being able to read.

* * * *

Batches spoke to many groups of parents about dyslexia. He would demonstrate, with his tutor, the approach used by the Center and talk about his life. Going over all that he had been through was painful. I asked him why he continued to do it and he replied, "If I can help just one person avoid going through what I went through in school, it is worth it."

* * * *

Mrs. Smith told her husband, "You are going to Parents' Night at the Center, and that is final." He replied, "All Steve needs to do is work harder. He got A's in middle school. There is no excuse for his failing grades in high school. Since you learned about different learners at the Center, you are just hoping that it is the cause of his failing grades. Steve is very intelligent. He needs to concentrate more on his studies and less on other things. It would be a waste of money to pay for tutoring, but to give you peace of mind, I will go."

As Batches was introduced as the speaker, Mr. Smith thought, 'Look at him. He can't even look at the audience. He looks at the floor.' However, the sincerity of Batches' voice as he talked about his life as a non-reader, all the ways he coped, his experiences in school, kept the father listening. As Batches continued, the father thought, 'He's describing

Steve. My son does some of those things when he reads. Maybe Steve does need help to improve his grades. Maybe all kids can't learn the same way.'

Steve received tutoring from the Center and his grades improved. The last I heard, Steve had attended college and was thinking about applying to law school.

* * * *

Unfortunately, although the means to teach dyslexics is available, the parents' ability to pay for that remediation often is not. Many parents who contacted the Center were unable to get help for their children because they could not afford the cost. Education should not depend on the ability to pay; education is a right which should not exclude the fifteen percent of the population who are dyslexic.

FOR PARENTS

CHAPTER 11

As the parent of a dyslexic, I have learned many things over the years, some of them by trial and error. Be aware that dyslexic children are labor intensive for parents.

As parents, how you treat your child is terribly important. Batches wasn't raised disabled. I remember the many times I worked with my son in his early elementary school years. I would say, 'Sit down. Do this. Concentrate. I know it's hard, but I know you can do it. Keep working at it.'

You need to praise your child. If they are trying very hard, and they are beginning to read better, you should say, "You did that very well. You are reading so much better. That was great." These children need all the positive reinforcement they can get. Don't say, "That word wasn't right." Gently say, "Could you read that again?" Often a dyslexic who misreads a word the first time will correct himself the next time.

You also need to allow your child to fail now and then. There are failures in everyone's life, and they need to learn how to cope with failure - but not failure after failure after unending failure.

Family understanding is very important. An old Chinese proverb says, 'Parents can give children two important things, roots and wings.'

* * * *

There are characteristics that dyslexic children exhibit in kindergarten of which you should be aware. These are normal occurrences at this stage. However, the non-dyslexic child will out grow these behaviors with time. The dyslexic child does not. One is the desire of some children to read and/or write from right to left instead of left to right. Another is mirror writing. They may write backwards, and if you hold the paper up to a mirror, you can read it properly in the reflection. They have difficulty sequencing. They may hear a story, and when they re-tell the story, they may put the beginning on the end and the middle at the beginning. They may have difficulty, as Batches did, stating the days of the week and months of the year in the correct order. Children like Batches have trouble learning to sound out letters of the alphabet. They have trouble with the phonemes (sounds). The graphemes (letters) they often can rattle off. They are good at singing their ABC's (sometimes out of order). When it comes to seeing these letters on a page and giving the correct sound they have difficulty.

Like Batches, they may have difficulty telling right from left. They may also be uncertain as to whether they are left handed or right handed (ambidexterity).

In the first grade, be aware that your child may be memorizing the words in their books. First grade books have lovely pictures. I've heard from parents whose children were reading like this. Neither the parents nor the teacher knew they were doing this, until they gave them a different book to read with the same words, and they couldn't read it. Even at this age, these bright children are trying to cope, so they don't look dumb.

Parents should also be aware at this age that the little words are troublesome to remember for someone with the problem of dyslexia. The following words: as, it, and, the, but, if, so, also; are very difficult for them to learn. These children confuse small words (the, as, and, but, in, on). They slide over longer words, often skipping them because they cannot pronounce them.

Your child's vocabulary may be limited, because they don't like to read. Parents, you need to read to them as much as possible, and have them look at the words as you read to expand your child's oral vocabulary. The libraries and Recordings for the Blind and Dyslexic also have books on tape - Treasure Island, Black Beauty, the classics - the RFBD will record just about any book requested. The greatest difficulty for a dyslexic is the processing of language both written and oral.

Ask your child to form a picture in her/his mind of what is being described in the reading. This helps with comprehension and memory skills. You can stop the tape or stop reading and ask your child to tell you what picture s/he has formed. This will tell you if your child needs to hear that part again, so they can form a better picture, and thus gain better comprehension. The techniques Visualizations and Verbalization that were developed into a curriculum by Nanci Bell teach readers to "make movies in their mind."

Your child may have difficulty processing oral directions. You might be giving him/her specific instructions such as: feed the dog; put feed in the birdfeeder; then wash your hands and set the table. Your child may come in after feeding the dog, sit down and start watching television. He isn't being naughty and ignoring what you said. He isn't being lazy, or just not wanting to comply. Do you say to him, "What are you doing? Didn't you hear me tell you to feed the dog, put feed in the birdfeeder, then wash your hands and set the table? Can't you remember anything? Are you stupid?" Your child is not stupid. He truly has difficulty processing lists, given to him orally. When he is small, you must learn to ask him to do one thing at a time. Then, as he gets older, you help him learn to do two things at a time, by having him repeat the two instructions that you gave him, back to you. When he gets much older and can read, you can write the lists down for him.

Some children have a problem with short-term memory. They cannot remember where they place things. Parents, you need to help them organize their room and organize their desk at school by showing them how to organize at home. Using a table, lay out their school books, pencils, crayons and glue, in a specific order, so they know exactly where to find them. Otherwise, they'll just stuff these things into their desk, and then won't be able to remember where they put them. My son learned this, to the point that when I cleaned his room, I placed everything I picked up exactly in the same place I had found it, or I heard about it. Dyslexics must learn to organize all the "tools" which they use and when finished replace them exactly where they were found.

I often wondered as a child why my father who was a carpenter was such a stickler about having his children replace all of his tools they used, in exactly the place they found them. I realize now that he possibly had a short-term memory problem, and he kept his tools in the exact same place, exactly like my son organizes his room now. With everything exactly in its place. My father did not waste time trying to find them.

Halfway through a sentence, your child may forget what s/he was going to say. They aren't dumb, or absent-minded. Their short-term memory weaknesses may have caused them to lose the second part of the sentence. Give them time to think of it, or use a word to trigger their memory.

Never finish a sentence for them. Let them converse with others. Don't speak for them.

In the third and fourth grade, you will begin to see your child read one word that looks like another word (could for would, become for because, dad for did). When they read, you may find they omit words, but not consciously. You may find them adding words to a sentence. You may find they leave off endings, such as -ing, -ly, -ed or -tion (slow for slowly, move for moving). Or they inappropriately may add these endings to words. These error patterns may change the entire meaning of a sentence. Dsylexics are working very hard to read, to concentrate on each word, and this affects their comprehension of what they are reading. If children are not taught to sound out small words, then larger words become more difficult for them to read.

Children with auditory processing problems may hear words differently. They may mistake words that sound alike (blue, instead of blow; ball, instead of bill). They may leave out, or add sounds to words (sighetti instead of spaghetti). It is also around this time in school, if they are not helped, that they begin to lose their self esteem.

Parents, you may see some of these characteristics concerning language processing in yourself, since it is often found in one or more members of a family.

When your child is in kindergarten, or early first grade, s/he may exhibit some of what I have described above. This may be a normal developmental stage. However, by the time a child has had a year in a traditional first grade, a parent may get tired of hearing that it's just a developmental stage they'll outgrow. The child may already be significantly behind in language processing. If a lower elementary school child of average or above cognitive ability has not learned to process language correctly after direct instruction in reading and spelling patterns, it is more than likely not just a developmental lag. Do not be patient in seeking help. Be assertive and decisive in seeking quality language assessment. Be sure that no physical problems exist by enlisting a pediatric ophthalmologist and an audiologist.

A person with dyslexia may be classified from severe to mild. My son was classified as a classic severe dyslexic. If a severe dyslexic, has not had the correct teaching of the structure of their language even by the end of first grade, s/he begins to get further and further behind in school work. The child becomes more and more discouraged with school. Children, who are classified as moderately dyslexic probably will be able to "keep up" and to cope, up until the fifth or sixth grade, depending on the severity of their problems. When reading and writing begin to play a much larger part of school work, they may have great difficulty. Dyslexics who are "mild" often survive without extreme difficulty through elementary, and middle school but may experience problems at the high school and college level. If they are strong, able listeners dyslexia may not affect their academic achievement to a point of causing falling grades until reading demands intensify.

Dyslexic's have their good and bad days. On good days, they seem to process well. Then, all of a sudden, they have a day when they can't process orally, they can't process written words, they can't process visually in their reading. They become very frustrated, or as Batches used to say, "flustrated." These children need adequate rest. They cannot process language when they are tired.

Another very important factor is their inability to cope with noise and distractions when they are trying to learn.

Any place they use to study needs to be free of noise. Extreme quiet, where they may read out loud and not bother others, or walk with their books, to feel the motion as they read, helps their processing. They also require frequent breaks, fifteen minutes in duration, because they are working very hard to process the language. Reading, spelling and writing are highly demanding cognitive tasks for a dyslexic.

Parents, do not expect these children to work in the same way that you work. Here's a typical example: You've sent your child out to rake the yard. You look out to see how he's doing. Surprise! He is not raking from one side of the yard to the other in a smooth pattern. He's worked in one area for a while and piled up the leaves. Now he's gotten tired of that and moved to another area of the yard and started to work. Your first impulse is to go out and tell him to do it your way. Don't. Eventually he will complete his chore, but not in your expected fashion. Accept and praise the completed task and the effort!

I know a mother who lived on a farm. She had taken her son out and taught him exactly how he should do his chores. She allowed herself to be driven up the wall because he did not do those chores in the exact way she had taught him. He did finish all the chores but in his own way. People are all unique and must be allowed and encouraged to find their own way.

* * * *

Should your child have difficulty with math, as is often the case with a dyslexic learner, you can be of help in many ways. Have your child count as s/he sets the table. Count each plate, spoon, knife and fork as it is set on the table.

Motion reinforces learning for dyslexics. There are many small chores that require counting, adding, and subtracting. Use your imagination to help your child learn his/her math skills.

Games with dice are excellent learning tools for math. Throwing them, adding, or counting the spots out loud all reinforce learning. Batches also found the abacus to be of great help. Again, the motion of moving the beads on the abacus back and forth helped him learn.

* * * *

If dyslexics cannot learn language visually, how can they learn living skills visually? They can't. These skills have to be consciously taught. I learned this lesson the hard way. At practically every-other meal, Batches would reach for his glass of milk or his cup of juice, and knock it over. Then came cleanup time for the entire table. This was an embarrassment to him. Finally unknowingly, I taught him this living skill. I said, "Batches, you're going to learn how to pick up a glass full of milk." I placed my hand on his right elbow. I said, "Open and extend all your fingers and your thumb. Now move your hand carefully, in this position, toward the glass until you touch the glass. When your hand is touching the glass, close your extended fingers carefully, but firmly, around the glass. Now lift." I had him repeat this action several times, and from that time on there were no more spills at breakfast, lunch or dinner. What a simple way to teach a simple task. However, at the time, I did not realize this was not a simple task for my child. An orderly sequence of steps helped him master an important task.

Batches and I went round and round before kindergarten when it was time for him to tie his shoe laces. He would have loved to have grown up in this day when it is considered cool for kids to run around with their shoelaces untied. When Batches was in school, they had to be tied, and he had to learn to tie. We worked at it and worked at it. He learned, but he hated to do it. There were many, many times I had to remind him, "Batches, please tie your shoelaces." I later learned, that part of his problem was fine motor coordination. Again it took from simple to complex, specific instructions, directly taught.

Parents, you need to consciously teach your child social skills. You need to teach them proper etiquette. Show them how to shake hands with a person when you meet, look them in the eye, then say, "Hello." Show them where to sit down when they walk into a room with several people in it. They need to be taught consciously how to behave. After a social situation, if your child has not done something correctly, recreate the scene. Then lead them through the situation again, this time instructing them in the correct way.

One of the instructors at the Center where Batches was tutored was especially. skilled in this area. She not only taught her students the language, she would also take them out to lunch and show them living skills they needed, or she might just go out for a Coke in the middle of a lesson. She walked through the social situation with the student, using verbal and visual reinforcement and repetition. These skills are taken for granted for most children who have good visual skills, but they are important skills that dyslexics must consciously learn.

Parents can help their dyslexic child by exposing them to the world and everyday experiences. Watch the education channels with your children. The Discovery Channel is fantastic. The color, the sound, the scenes, the movement - it was easier for my son to learn from these programs that were enriching and enlivening to his senses.

* * * *

Your child could be the star of the basketball or football or soccer team. How did they learn to remember those plays? Through motion and touch. Yet they struggle to remember history facts for a test. Try having your child hold a miniature football/basketball as s/he studies history facts. During the test have your child hold the same football/basketball. Your child may recall history facts in the same manner s/he recalls important basketball strategies, by touch and motion.

Your child could have rhythmic intelligence. One intelligent student had taken the EMT licensing test twice and had failed. She had also failed High School, but she knew she would be a good emergency medical technician. I sat down with her and asked her what she thought her strengths were. One of them was music. She loved to sing and could remember all the lyrics of most songs but could not pass the 'stupid' test. I asked her to create a rhythm in her head. I told her that when she studied for the exam to recite all the facts to herself using that rhythm. I told her that when she took her test to recite the questions to herself using the same rhythm. Not out loud of course. I'm happy to report that she passed her test!

You need to think outside of the box when it comes to educating your child. If your child loves to play ball with his/her friends, most parents would say "you can play for an hour, then you have to come inside to study for your biology test." Instead you could try setting up a play-time study group. Each child taking a turn teaching the others. The motion and touch of playing while studying may be just the method that helps your child learn.

Your child may be struggling with spelling tests. Have your child practice by typing the words slowly instead of writing them with a pencil. When s/he is taking the test at school, if s/he can't remember a word, have them stop and pretend the desk is a keyboard and see if by touching the desk in the same way they touched the keyboard, s/he remembers how to spell the word.

* * * *

Parents, you need to learn all you can about dyslexia. You must be knowledgeable about the subject. The fact that legally your child has a right to be taught in the way s/he can learn will guide your search. You must be able to discuss the signs and characteristics of dyslexia. When you approach school personnel, firmly but gently, with complete knowledge of the subject, they may listen to you. If you are not heard the first time, or the second, don't give up. Include other parents of dyslexics in your efforts. Support each other. **You are the front line for change in our public schools!**

If you do not have the skills or confidence to successfully advocate for your child, you need to call in a professional child advocate. Each state should have a professional advocate available through Child Protection and Advocacy Services or similar advocacy agency. You need to request that an advocate investigate your child's situation and represent your child in meetings with school administrators.

* * * *

Here are several books that I recommend parents read. You can find them at the public library:

Cordoni, Barbara. Living With a Learning Disability, Southern Illinois University Press, Carbondale and Edwardsville, IL, 1987.

Evans, James. 1983. An Uncommon Gift, The Westminster Press,Philadelphia.

MacCracken, Mary. 1986. Turnabout Children, Overcoming Dyslexia and Other Learning Disabilities, Little Brown and Co., Boston.

Silver, Larry, M.D. 1984. The Misunderstood Child: A Guide for Parents of Learning Disabled Children, McGraw-Hill Publishing Co.

Vail, Priscilla L. 1990. About Dyslexia: Unraveling the Myth, Modern Learning Press/Programs for Education, Rosemont, N.J.

* * * *

If your child is having great difficulty in learning the language by the end of first grade, it is essential that you seek a knowledgeable professional to do a proper evaluation. Make sure the Evaluator or Evaluative team has been versed in the characteristics of dyslexia. Make sure the testing is indepth and includes a battery such as: Woodcock Reading Mastery Tests; Detroit Tests of Learning Aptitude; Wide Range Achievement Test III, Revised; Gray-Oral Reading Tests - 3; Written Paragraph (informal); Test of Written Language - Revised; Blending Drill; Bender-Gestalt (shows what the child actually sees); and Clinical Evaluation of Language Fundamentals (CELF) - Revised (measures auditory processing). Various sub-tests are available to assess specific auditory skills. The Wechsler Intelligence Scale, if used by an expert, will show functional intelligence, not the true intelligence of a dyslexic. However, it differentiates left and right brain function which can be helpful in evaluating a dyslexic. Performance Verbal and Full Scale intelligence quotients are necessary. Fundamental to any quality language evaluation for dyslexia is a measure of phoneme awareness. The Lindamood Auditory conceptualization test (LAC) or Phoneme Awareness Inventories also exist.

When you meet with the Evaluator to review your child's tests, make sure you leave with a thorough understanding of what characteristics of language learning differences are involved in your child's specific case. What are the child's strong skill areas? What are the child's areas of difficulty/ weakness? [Word comprehension; auditory and visual processing; written expression; short-term and long-term memory difficulties; word attack; spelling; reading configuratively (one word that looks like another); omissions; repetitions; mispronunciations; and underlying poor phonemic awareness.]

Parents, you need to know what is in your child's school records. Do not allow a report from any Evaluator that says, "This child does not have the ability/IQ to learn" to be included in your child's school records. Since 1974, federal law requires parents to be part of a committee along with school personnel - general education teacher of child, coordinator of special needs, appropriate special education teacher, school principal and psychological/educational evaluator - to build a three-year plan of education action for a child (0-26 years old). The Individual Educational Plan (IEP) is reviewed every year. The evaluation information is updated every three years. If parents are not satisfied with the original committee information and/or educational plan, they may request further testing and a new committee.

A learning disability as fundamental as dyslexia deserves a second opinion. Besides in-school psychoeducational evaluations, many wise, educated parents seek a private, independent test battery for dyslexia. Agencies such as the "Thirty-Second Degree Masonic Learning Centers for Children," knowledgeable hospitals and dyslexia-specific clinics will offer comprehensive diagnostic language evaluations and thorough written reports with recommendations for home and school.

Parents, you need to make sure that your child's teacher has been trained in the Orton-Gillingham Kinesthetic Tactile approach. Orton-Gillingham worked for Batches and millions of other learners world-wide. I also need to mention that there are other excellent multisensory structured language education approaches (MSLE).

* * * *

According to Michigan State Law #340.1747 no more than ten students should be in a special education classroom at a time, with no more than a fifteen student case load for the teacher. Regular classroom size is according to contractual agreement with teachers in individual public schools. Parents, we need to demand adequate staffing levels at schools to meet our children's needs. Some classrooms have too many students. How can teachers meet students needs? How can teachers be aware of students' problems? By having a manageable number of students in the classroom and by having teachers trained to meet the needs of the children they are teaching, the needs of students can be better met. Both students and teachers can grow and thrive.

* * * *

Parents, you need to demand that changes take place within our educational bureaucracy. It is your child's right to be taught language skills by the approach which allows successful learning. Teaching style must match the learning style. This makes perfect, logical, ethical sense.

Sometimes I lie awake at night wondering what is going to happen to the dyslexics who are in our school system. I wonder how dyslexics can become better understood by our society. I've lain in bed and listened to the Larry King talk show. I have heard him several times hang up on a caller who was too slow in stating their question or point. I wonder how many of these callers are dyslexic and may be slower at processing what they want to say. Have patience, world. The creative question, idea or thought from the dyslexic might just be the one this world needs. Where would we be without Thomas Edison who was sent home by a teacher because he was unteachable, or Albert Enstein? Dyslexics often have gifted minds.

FOR EDUCATORS

CHAPTER 12

Dyslexic children, after being tested by the School Psychologist, are frequently put into learning disabled classrooms in public schools. Learning disabled classrooms, in our public schools need to be restructured. The learning disabled classroom classification suggests that a child is **unable to learn in the standard way**. People have lost sight of this classification. People believe learning disabled, means unable to learn. Schools need to restructure classrooms for the learning disabled, so that all children can learn.

Learning disabled classrooms are supposedly funded by the government, but the government funding is inadequate. Children with different strengths, weaknesses and intellect, are put together in the same learning disabled classroom. Children in our schools need indepth testing and interpretation, thereof, by knowledgeable diagnosticians. Then, they need to be placed in a classroom that will match their specific learning style. Intelligent dyslexics need to be in classrooms that will help strengthen their language weaknesses and challenge their non-language intellect. They need to express creativity and ideas, as well as learn organizational skills. Another dyslexic may have a different set of language weaknesses. They need to be in a different classroom, but they still need a creative outlet.

Children's learning styles are different, yet most public school systems offer parents two options - one) a mainstream education classroom, or two) a learning disabled classroom. Our schools need several different types of classrooms because children have different learning styles.

Mainstreaming older dyslexic children who were not identified as 'at risk to learn' at a young age does not work.

Unfortunately, school children have learned not to be accepting of peers who are different. They make fun of children who need to arm tap to learn to spell. In turn, dyslexic children are afraid of appearing different in front of their classmates. Dyslexic children need to be in an environment where successful learning can take place. Otherwise, they will struggle and struggle, as my son did.

Children learn differently. All of us must understand that learning disabled does not mean stupid and develop curricula and materials accordingly. Learning disabled means, unable to learn in the standard way. This is not connected to intelligence. Children and teachers must be taught to be accepting of diversity and actually be surprised that any two learners are alike.

One school system in my area has made these changes. They have special kindergarten and elementary classes for those children who have been determined to be "at risk" for language learning. These classes are taught by teachers who are trained in the Orton-Gillingham Kinesthetic Tactile approach. However, there was nothing beyond elementary school for these children in this school system, at the time I wrote this book.

The multisensory structured language education approaches are somewhat geographically based. For example, Orton-Gillingham is widely used in the Eastern part of the United States. In the Southern U.S., in Texas, for instance, multisensory programs follow the alphabetic phonics approach. Importantly, however, there is now standardization of content and Principles of Instruction among the myriad MSLE programs. Quality programs require the trainers to have rich educational backgrounds and extensive teaching experience with language-disabled individuals. Trainees, also, are carefully screened, taught, and overseen in the field by Trainers and Master Teachers.

I would like to see all school systems teach children, who are "at risk" to learn, with the Orton-Gillingham Kinesthetic Tactile approach. After kindergarten, in the first and second grades, they could combine the "at risk" students, and continue teaching them their language skills with this multisensory structured language education approach. Children who begin their academic career learning by this approach can often learn in a regular classroom that is attuned to their language needs. Non-dyslexic children in the classroom need to be accepting of diversity, and the dyslexic children need to be given time to process language. Students, who are more severely affected, would need special one-on-one instruction in school. One-on-one tutoring would be another added expense to already overburdened public school systems; however if this country is really committed to ending illiteracy, it is a necessity. Government funding should be provided. There should be a language instructor available for these children all the way through high school to meet their needs. Since dyslexia is of constitutional origin which means it has been present since birth, the brain must be trained as it is, changes must be in the teaching style and material used for those with these wonderfully unique brain configurations.

* * * *

There are many recommendations that teachers can apply to a regular classroom that will not only teach dyslexics but also the children that are not dyslexic.

Instruction in reading should be simultaneously multi-sensory in it's approach. The use of motion, touch, sight and sound should all be incorporated into the instruction. The teaching of reading should be structured from the simple to the complex. It should be a step-by-step (small-incremental) teaching, with the opportunity for much repetition, much review, and re-teaching. **Over-learning is essential at every stage.**

Tapes, or records with phonics played rhythmically are highly recommended. Large wooden letters should be available so children can touch the outline of the letters and learn how they feel. Sand trays can be made available in classrooms for children to trace and write in. (Parents can make a "sand" tray at home for children to use by taking a cookie sheet and putting dry jello in it. But don't be surprised if their finger goes into their mouth between letters.) Play sand is used in most classrooms and language therapy sessions, since it provides rough tactili that helps children learn sound/letter combinations.

Ask your students to repeat back to you classroom expectations and assignments. That way, you can find out if they understood and have processed correctly what you told them or what was written. Make sure the dyslexic student understands what kind of behavior is expected in class (when they can talk to classmates, when they have to work silently).

Find a place where a student can read out loud without disturbing other students. A dyslexic who processes auditorially needs to hear his/her own voice in order to help place class material into long-term memory. It is also good for a dyslexic to be read to, often by another student. This should be a positive time for both the dyslexic and the reader.

Never ask a dyslexic to read out loud to the class, unless they specifically ask to do so.

Dyslexics need adequate time to process information. Tests should not be timed if one wants a reliable assessment of a dyslexic's knowledge. When children are tested on their multiplication tables, they are given two or three minutes to complete them. What is wrong with giving a child ten minutes to complete a test to find out if that child knows their multiplication tables? Are we such a "hurry-up society" today, that we cannot allow these children who do not process as quickly as others the time they need without penalizing them in some way? Can't we give them the time they need to be able to show their teacher what they actually know and have learned? A timed math test shows only how many facts you know in that amount of time. It does not show how many math facts the student really knows. Processing and production time are of essence to a dyslexic learner.

Dyslexics need to learn organizational skills. Having a set daily routine that is legibly written out and placed on the board or on the student's desk is important. Some dyslexics have problems with short-term memory and need to have consistency to organize and store information in long-term memory. Short-term memory means that you may have spent time yesterday going over a specific problem with your students, and the next day, you are ready to go on. However, the dyslexic student has forgotten yesterday's information and cannot understand today's problem. The information is not in his/her short-term memory to build on in this situation. Study guides are enormously helpful in reinforcing learning.

When an all written test is given, and a dyslexic student has difficulty writing; this test becomes a test on writing. It is not a test of what the student knows about a particular subject. Sometimes oral tests are needed to find out what a dyslexic knows. Only one of Batches' high school teachers allowed him to take his tests orally. The playing field was not at all level for Batches.

Allowances must be made for the student's written work by giving them additional time to produce. You may have to expect less in terms of quantity. It would be helpful if dyslexics could write on wide lined paper, every other line (double spaced). It would also be appropriate, to permit the dyslexic to underline all the words they perceive as being misspelled without deducting points. This would accentuate the positive and allow them to build vital self-esteem. They must find success with their acquired knowledge of a subject. Praise for the things in which they excel sustains them through the rough times. Can't we all relate to this?

Spelling words should be written down on separate cards with a picture of what the word represents next to it. The dyslexic will pull up the picture from memory (to them it is like a diagram) and the word will be attached to it. For example, steal would have a picture of someone taking something next to the word, and the letter a would be colored; steel would have a picture of iron next to the word, and the letter e would be highlighted in another color. The differing color differentiates the spelling. Save the color red for the words such as of and from, which are not able to be analyzed by sound.

Placing dyslexic students close to you at the front of the class can help them concentrate. There will be fewer distractions. The students would be able to look at you while you are teaching. This is also an advantage for students who are taping their lessons, because your voice will sound clearer.

No negative connotations should be attached to this close placement where the learner really needs to be.

When math assignments are required, let the students do them on graph paper. This will help them keep the columns straight. It is also good for them to do frequent hands on counting, with lots of motion and touching while they count.

Remember, dyslexic children are working very hard to process. They need to take frequent breaks. Short "bursts" of study are more productive for all learners; dyslexics need every consideration and deserve such shorter periods of study.

* * * *

I know there has been progress made since Batches went to public school. I know that some school systems in this country are trying to meet the needs of dyslexic children. During the summer, some elementary school teachers take a two or three week, intensive course, to learn the Orton-Gillingham Kinesthetic Tactile approach used by the Center. Forty-five class hours with a 100 hour supervised practicum is recommended.

One of the teachers went back to her classroom in September, and began to teach one of her students using this approach. The child was repeating first grade, as she was having great difficulty learning to read. Just before Thanksgiving, this teacher went running down the school's hallway, excitedly calling to the other teachers in their rooms, "It works. It works. She's reading. It works!" This bright, intelligent little girl was reading, because she was being taught by a style of construction that was compatible to her learning style.

My hope is that this book will inspire other teachers to try this way of teaching language skills. I realize there is a long road ahead to reach all dyslexic children. My goal is that all children receive a good education, and one day can say to their mothers, as Batches said to me, **"It's amazing what you can learn when you can read."**

We all know that this is true. Reading opens the doors to learning. As we make a commitment to our parents, students, teachers and all of society to finally unlock the doors to literacy. Dyslexia will mean dys - difficulty, lexia - language. A difficulty that will be overcome! The time is right, the time is now!

* * * *

Here are several books that I recommend teachers read.

Adams, Marilyn Jager. 1990 Beginning to Read - A Summary. Cambridge: Reading Research and Education Center, University of Illinois, Champaign (Cat. 5078).

Birsch, Judith. Multisensory Teaching of Basic Language Skills. Brooks Publishers (1999). Baltimore, MD (Chapters 1-9).

Bowen, Carolyn C., E.P.S. Angling For Words.

Clark, Diana Brewster and Uhry, Joanna Kellogg. 1995. Dyslexia: Theory and Practice of Remedial Instruction. Baltimore, MD: York Press (1992) (Cat. 5075).

Gillingham, Anna and Stillman, Bessie. 1997. The Gillingham Manual Remedial Training for Children. Cambridge.

Henry, Marcia, E.P.S. Words.

Rome, Paula and Osman, Jean. Language Took Kit Manuel.

Traub, Nina, E.P.S. Recipe For Reading.

FOR COLLEGE STUDENTS

CHAPTER 13

In college, dyslexics need to advocate for themselves. Dyslexia is listed as a disability in Public Law 94-142 signed by President George Bush. It is important for these students, to sign up at their college's special needs services office. Their civil rights are protected in Section 504 of our law. I can not stress enough the importance of this action. This will help these students, even students who had good grades in high school. Students with mild dyslexia may not start to have problems until college. They know they are smart but don't understand why they are not achieving as well as they should be in college. After they have a full language skills assessment, they will be aware of their individual strategies for successful learning. These students will then understand their own learning style and will be able to explain their strengths and weaknesses to others. They must ask for what they need; therefore, they must be allowed to know what they need.

College students need to approach their professors and tell them they have dyslexia. They need to tell the professor that they have the right to tape their classes. Dyslexics have a right to use an electric spell checker and any tools necessary to improve their learning ability. Most importantly, they need time to complete tests with absolutely no set time limit. Batches got a little tired of having to tell the professor that he was dyslexic, and he was registered at the special needs office, but it was the best thing for him to do. He was given all the time he needed to complete tests. He was allowed to use the recordings for the Blind and Dyslexic and also his own tapes of his classes.

Batches used a highlighter to highlight the important factors in his books. He frequently reviewed his tapes of lectures and books to help his memory. He needed to be very organized with his books, tapes and handouts. He wasn't shy about asking for help from his professor - not at the last minute before the exam, but early in the semester. He also took advantage of choosing the pass-fail option, whenever possible, to avoid the added pressure of a letter grade. He was consistent about studying in the same place where there were no distractions. (This may be difficult for students who live in a dorm.) He was consistent about going to class and being on time, sitting in the same place in the classroom, preferably the front row. He needed to study at a time when his concentration was the best, taking frequent breaks.

Batches found the community college to be very supportive of people with this specific language disability. The classes were small; the professor's were very caring. Batches was able to have his needs met. Even at larger campuses, students need to advocate and develop relationships with other students, so they can have a study partner who has strengths in areas where they are weak. Interacting with other students, helps them verbalize their ideas, a kind of rehearsal. It helps them be better prepared for class.

At the beginning of each term, Batches would xerox off three months of a large calendar. He would write in the boxes - exam in life science, paper due in psychology, chapter two due in psychology, etc. Then he would put the calendar side-by-side. This gave him a visual outline of the timeframe for the term in which he was working. This was very helpful in enabling him to break down long term tasks into small steps. Then he would stick to the schedule.

One of Batches' professors found something very unusual about the way in which dyslexics take an objective test. He noted to Batches, after he had graded his first test, that Batches had missed questions that he felt that Batches had known. Batches informed the instructor that the two sheet exam (one with the questions, one to write the answers) was very confusing for him. It seems, that in looking down to find the proper answer as A, B, or C, and then going from that sheet to the answer sheet, he often transposed A to B or 1 to 2. Of course, the answer is graded as wrong. The instructor who understood about dyslexia agreed that on the next test, Batches should use the question sheet instead of the answer sheet to mark his answers. By doing this, the results were fantastic. Batches did much, much better simply by being allowed to use the question sheet which omitted an extra language processing step.

Batches became what he laughingly called, "the electric student." He took a voice controlled tape recorder to his classes and taped all of his lectures. His father and I also purchased the Franklin Language Master LM 2000 for Batches. This particular speller uses batteries and contains the Merriam-Webster dictionary. Batches had assimilated sufficient language skills that he could spell a word well enough that the Franklin Speller would recognize the word and then spell it for him correctly. Not only did it spell the word, but it also gave the definition of the word. It also gave him synonyms. This speller is an instrument that is a must for all dyslexics to use.

* * * *

Receiving a college education was once out of reach for many dyslexics. They did not have the support system to make it. Today, dyslexics should not be ashamed that they learn differently; they must advocate at all times and in all classes. It will educate college professors and personnel to the problems a dyslexic has in the academic system. Dyslexics need to step forward and thus, future dyslexic students might be assured of college professors who understand this unique style of language-based learning.

VISUAL TOOL

CHAPTER 14

I have discovered another tool that Batches uses to help him read. Some dyslexics, also have a problem known as 'scotopic sensitivity syndrome.' The reflection of light off white paper, with black lettering, causes some people not to be able to see the print clearly. In some instances, the print will appear to move around on the paper. In some instances, the print will be blurred. In many instances, the stress of fighting the dyslexia and coping with the scotopic sensitivity slows the person's reading to the point where it takes many hours to read a few pages.

Helen Irlen started the research on scotopic sensitivity syndrome. She came up with the idea of testing individuals with different colored transparencies. She put these transparencies over the white sheet of paper with black lettering. A client would then be asked to choose the color that allowed them to see the words clearly. The color that would stop the words from moving on the page. She could tell by the speed in which they read the words back to her which color was best for them. The client would take this color sheet home to use experimentally for a few weeks to see if it helped them improve their reading. The transparencies were never described as a cure for dyslexia but rather a means by which light sensitivity and glare interference caused by the black print on stark white paper could be reduced.

Having heard of this, and noting that I had often walked into a room at sundown and told Batches, "Turn on the lights; how can you see to read?" I had Batches tested in Chicago. The evaluation showed Batches had problems with scotopic sensitivity. He was fitted with a pair of non-prescription, specially tinted glasses.

People who have trouble driving at night when the lights from the oncoming cars blind them may have scotopic sensitivity. Batches always complained about driving at night. He also read better with the lights out. People who tire easily when they read, and also complain of headaches even though a regular eye exam shows no problem may have scotopic sensitivity.

After Batches had been using his glasses for a while, he came downstairs one day and said, "It's nice to be able to see more than one word at a time when I read." Professors will say there has not been enough research done on these glasses to qualify them as helpful for people to use. This may be true. However, my only response to these professors is Batches' response, "It's nice to be able to see more than one word at a time when I read." This statement made me realize that the lenses he wears are another valuable tool to assist in the reading process. This is not to say that I do not value research. However, in this specific situation, my common sense told me, 'Use it.'

These glasses are expensive. For those who need help for scotopic sensitivity, there is a less-expensive option. Continue using the colored transparencies until funds are available for the glasses.

EPILOGUE

Everyone wants a happy ending for these different learners. However, this doesn't always occur. I have seen dyslexics at the Center, not as severe as Batches, give up. They become discouraged when they find their learning struggles don't go away. Some don't want to work hard to learn - at least not as hard as they must to really acquire vital skills. A few find it easy to fall back on old patterns of living.

On May 2, 1992 Batches received his Bachelors in Applied Arts degree from a state university. That joyous Saturday, the weather was hot and hazy, as we drove up to the university. The type of day to have commencement in a large airy stadium. However, as we got close to the stadium, we could see a line of people going into the student events center. "They can't be holding graduation inside, can they?" Sure enough they did. The weather bureau said the nasty storms on radar could move into the area.

We parked the car, and the four of us sat looking at our two tickets. My sister and my daughter said they would watch graduation on the big screen TV that was provided. Batches' girlfriend and I headed for the arena. As we walked down the hallway toward the arena people holding tickets in their hands, came towards us. It was obvious that the arena was full. They were not letting anymore people in, even those with tickets. I squared my shoulders and kept walking towards the door. Batches' girlfriend was right behind me. She saw the set of my shoulders and knew there was going to be trouble. Thinking fast, as we reached the door, before anyone could open their mouth, she said, "People are holding our seats for us. We already have seats, but we had to go to the restroom before it started." The man at the door let us in.

It had been twenty-one years since Batches last graduation and ten years since he returned home from Arizona, dejected. Again there were strangers in the crowd, who didn't know, or understand what it had cost Batches to make it there. This time there was no cartwheel.

Batches climbed his mountain to the very top. Through dedication, determination, a desire to learn, plus his family's support, he reached his goal. My miracle happened.

* * * *

There were many people who helped Batches. Margaret and Harry Foster who had the vision to see the need for a Dyslexia Center were the first. Mr. Foster passed away on March 11, 1996. Mary Lee Killingbeck, who was Director of the Center when Batches attended lessons and who not only taught Batches his language skills but other life skills and became his friend. I considered her to be one of the best, if not the best, instructor in the Orton-Gillingham Kinesthetic Tactile approach. Mary Lee died August 22, 1998 of ovarian cancer at the age of 49 knowing both "the challenge and the promise" of Dyslexia. She lived in the shoes of a dyslexic and walked the path with other dyslexics. Her life taught the true lessons of struggle and success. Dr. Alice Hamachek provided tutoring once Batches reached college level reading.

There were many others at the Center who also contributed to his success. Cam tutored him in algebra. Sandy taught him computer skills. Dutch searched out interesting books for him to read. And Eugenia cared about all dyslexics. My thanks go to all of these, plus others too numerous to name.

* * * *

Publishing my book has not been an easy task. It has been nine years since I first wrote it. Amy K. White became the Executive Director of the Dyslexia Resource Center in Howell, Michigan after Mary Lee. She is a former public school teacher, and a Language Evaluator and Language Therapist for the Center. Her adjunct title was actually Therapy Level Trainer as the Dyslexia Resource Center in Howell provided teachers training and practica for other Centers in Michigan. New Michigan Center's are in Detroit, Bay City, and Grand Rapids, other Masonic Centers with which the Dyslexia Resource Center worked are in Toledo, Ohio and Fort Wayne, Indiana. The above are all under the umbrella of the Title of "Thirty-Second Degree Masonic Learning Centers for Children."

Jo Ann Hunziker was Co-trainer with Amy White at the Howell Center. JoAnn helped provide training for those who want to do private tutoring. She also helped train public school teachers who saw the Center's students improving in their language skills.

* * * *

Unfortunately the Dyslexia Resource Center in Howell, Michigan was forced to close it's doors in 2002, a casualty of the economy. Fortunately Amy White is still working in the field of educating teachers and the Center's tutors are still working with their students.

* * * *

Matching teaching style to learning style requires that teachers know the rules and structural patterns of the English language. We must sustain and expand the effort to train teachers, parents, and school administrators, all of whom have a vested interest in the fate of all learners. **Because it really is amazing what you can learn when you can read!**

About the Author

Magdalene Wilson was born in Waldo, Ohio in 1921. She graduated with honors from Ohio State University in 1943 with a degree in education. She taught high school science and physical education and had almost earned her Master's degree at Ohio State when she married in 1949 and moved to East Lansing, Michigan to raise a family. Her struggle to educate her intelligent son has led her to see the need to educate parents and teachers. It is her hope that present day educators will see the merit of her ideas and value her suggestions.